Expert

Professor Roger Kneebone directs the Imperial College Centre for Engagement and Simulation Science and the Royal College of Music–Imperial College Centre for Performance Science. His first career was as a surgeon, operating on trauma patients in southern Africa. He then changed direction, becoming a general practitioner in south-west England. Now, as an academic at Imperial College London, he researches what experts from different fields can learn from one another. His unorthodox and creative team includes clinicians, computer scientists, musicians, magicians, potters, puppeteers, tailors and fighter pilots. This is his first book for a general readership.

Expert

Understanding the Path to Mastery

ROGER KNEEBONE

VIKING

an imprint of

PENGUIN BOOKS

VIKING

UK | USA | Canada | Ireland | Australia
India | New Zealand | South Africa

Viking is part of the Penguin Random House group of companies
whose addresses can be found at global.penguinrandomhouse.com.

First published 2020
001

Copyright © Roger Kneebone, 2020

The publisher is grateful for permission to use the following: on pp. 91–2,
extract from *Zen and the Art of Motorcycle Maintenance* by Robert Pirsig © 1974, on p. 129,
extract from *The Spaces Between Us* by Michael Graziano © 2018, on pp. 236–7,
extract from *The Nature and Art of Workmanship* by David Pye © 1968, on pp. 291–2,
extract from *A Guide for the Perplexed* by E. F. Schumacher © 1977

Set in 14.71/17.63 pt Garamond MT Std
Typeset by Jouve (UK), Milton Keynes
Printed and bound in Great Britain by Clays Ltd, Elcograf S.p.A.

A CIP catalogue record for this book is available from the British Library

HARDBACK ISBN: 978–0–241–39203–4
TRADE PAPERBACK ISBN: 978–0–241–39204–1

www.greenpenguin.co.uk

To Dusia

Contents

APPRENTICE | JOURNEYMAN | MASTER

PASSING
IT ON

'IT'S NOT
ABOUT YOU'

DOING
TIME

USING YOUR
SENSES

DEVELOPING
VOICE

SPACE AND
OTHER PEOPLE

1. Experts and invisible fish

When I visited Derek Frampton, he was posing a clouded leopard. I'd never seen a clouded leopard before. She was sitting like a cat, her tail curled round her, gazing at a tiny cub which looked as if it was about to run away and play. They were so realistic I could hardly believe they were stuffed.

Derek is a taxidermist, one of the best there is. He'd invited me to his house to see how he works. We were in his 'display room', full to bursting with animals of every kind. Glass cases of birds and reptiles, every surface covered with creatures. On one table was a parakeet nearing completion, its wings held in position by threads; on another was an alligator with its jaws about to snap shut, next to a tree frog glowing like a jewel in the sunlight. Apart from the eerie stillness, it was like being in a menagerie.

I'd arranged to visit Derek because he's one of the country's leading experts in his field. I'm interested in experts and I wanted to find out more. Moving a half-finished skink from a chair so I could sit down, Derek explained what taxidermy involves.

He made the process sound pretty straightforward. You remove the animal's skin, recreate its body shape with a plaster model and place the skin over the model. He showed me a zebra's hide, shapeless and slumped in a corner. When I asked how he would create the plaster shape for those final stages, he said, 'Well, you just sculpt a zebra that size and put the skin back on.'

It's that 'just' that's key. If you want a zebra, you *just* sculpt one that size. It's obvious. But to me it isn't obvious, it's unimaginable. It's what makes Derek an expert.

Taxidermy is not a science, a craft or an art, Derek told me. It's a practice which combines all three. The science is in the precision, close observation and accuracy which allow his work to be a reference point for scientific research. Zoologists may refer to Derek's specimens for years to come, so the precise details of a mammal's colouring, a fish's scales or a reptile's teeth might be crucial in identifying new species or tracking the decline of animal populations. The craft is in the skills Derek has built up throughout his career: his ability to take the skin off an animal, then recreate that specimen's unique shape in plaster or wax. And the art is what brings it all together, making that clouded leopard look as if she's about to stoop down and lick her little cub. It's because he's an expert that Derek can combine these strands, applying them with wisdom and care to each new situation. Becoming expert is what this book is about.

Becoming expert

I'm a doctor. Medicine, too, is not a science, a craft or an art, but a practice which combines all three. Of course it is founded on science, that factual knowledge I spent so long studying as a student. The craft is how I worked as a practitioner, examining patients, operating on them or talking with them in my consulting room. The art is how I made sense of each patient and the problems they brought to me. The connection between Derek and me might not seem obvious at first, since surely taxidermy and medicine are completely different worlds. But that's not the case at all.

After explaining the basics, Derek took me into his workshop, which was like an alchemist's laboratory. The room was full of works in progress and there were all sorts of animals – birds and mammals, fish and reptiles. Creatures large and small, at every stage of preparation. An edible dormouse was on his workbench, a gorilla's head hung on the wall, and an antelope's torso stood in a corner. The air smelled of glue and plaster, and gurgling noises came from the next room.

In the centre of the room was the wooden cabinet where Derek keeps his most precious tools, the ones he inherited from his master. He only has a few and he's been using them for decades. The cabinet is the size of a wind-up gramophone and has two brass-handled drawers. On top is a turntable, where a tiny clay frog lay next to some of Derek's sculpting instruments. Rotating the turntable slowly by hand, Derek can work on specimens like that frog without damaging them. All around are the materials he needs. His workshop is where the science, craft and art come together.

Derek has been a taxidermist for forty-five years, mounting ('setting up', he calls it) everything from giraffes to shrews, from Komodo dragons to fish. He's in high demand by museums, zoos and private collectors. Though much of his work is with new specimens, he also conserves examples from scientific collections of animals and birds that are now disappearing or even extinct. Expert taxidermists, like many of the animals they work with, are rare creatures indeed.

I asked Derek how he started his career. At school, he told me, he loved art. He was good with his hands but he's dyslexic and he found studying difficult. When he was twelve he came across a dead blackbird on the road, took it home and started to draw it. He was fascinated by the bird's anatomy, by the delicate mechanism of its wings. From then on, he collected as many dead animals as his mother would let him get away with, drawing and painting them as accurately as he could. His epiphany, as he described it, came when he was sixteen. One day he realized that he didn't have to draw these animals as he found them; instead, he could pose them. He never looked back. He joined the Natural History Museum in London as an apprentice taxidermist, working there for many years before striking out on his own.

Not everyone can become an expert taxidermist like Derek. Not everyone would want to. Yet finding out how Derek and others like him in different fields have become so expert is relevant to all of us. What does it mean to *be* an expert? How do you become one? What makes Derek an *expert*, rather than just someone who is very good at what he does?

We can all become expert at something, though we probably can't become really expert in more than one or two areas. To become an expert you have to concentrate on your selected field, pushing distractions aside and focusing intently for year after year. It's a long, demanding process that takes great effort, and there's a lot of frustration along the way. This sounds obvious, but it's something people often overlook. We live in a world that demands immediate results. We are also taught to believe that talent is innate, and that if you don't show flair for something, it isn't worth pursuing. I don't think either of those things is true. Moving along the path towards becoming expert brings its own rewards: the slow march towards mastery is deeply satisfying – and, as we'll discover, it meets a fundamental human need. Besides which, you won't find out how talented you are until you try.

This book

This book is about experts and what it is to become one. I've been fascinated by experts for as long as I can remember. I've spent years watching them, talking to them, working with them, thinking about them, learning from them and marvelling at them. In the last few years I've made this a focus of my university teaching and research. I've read what others have written and I've explored theories of how people become expert, whether as an individual or in a group. I've spent countless hours with some of the world's leading experts in many different fields. I've tried to fathom what makes them what they are. Throughout all of this, it's the people who have caught my imagination – not 'expertise' in an abstracted sense, but the experts themselves.

Having expertise is one thing. *Being expert* is another. Am I an expert? It probably looks that way from the outside. It's over forty years since I qualified as a doctor. As I'll explain in the next chapter, since then I trained as a consultant surgeon and spent years operating on patients in the UK and South Africa. Then for nearly two decades I was a family doctor in a country town in the south-west of England. Now I'm a professor at Imperial College London, where I divide my time between teaching and research, much of it about experts. But I don't *feel* expert. To me it seems as if I'm just beginning to make sense of all that experience. Having said that, many experts I've spoken to describe a similar feeling.

Much of what experts do is invisible, even to themselves. Being expert is about how you think and see things. It's the result of an internal process that establishes who you are; it's not simply defined by what you create. We seldom see *how* experts become expert. We might experience what they make or do, but we don't see how they got there. We watch someone perform a trumpet solo in a concert hall, but we don't see the lifetime of practice behind their flawless execution. When we look at a painting in a gallery, we're not seeing the thousands of studies that led to it. But if you want to be an expert, you have to go through a long process. This book describes that process.

I've tried to work out what makes experts expert. I've tried to put into words their apparent ease, their mastery of materials, their instinctive judgement, their ways of knowing and doing, and their ability to respond to the unexpected. I've tried to capture their commitment to something beyond themselves. This is a tall order. Being expert is something you do, not something you describe. Much of it is impossible to put into words. It's only when you've tried to do their work yourself that you get a sense of how skilled such experts really are. Theirs is the art that conceals art.

It's like the apocryphal story of the elderly boiler-maker who is hired to fix a heating system that has stopped working. He arrives at the site, asks a few questions, listens to the system, takes out a hammer from his overalls and gives a sharp tap to one of the pipes. The system starts working and he goes home. The whole thing has taken a few minutes. Then he sends a bill for £500. The client is outraged at being charged so much for just using a hammer and asks him to itemize the bill. He replies: 'For use of hammer: £5. For knowing where to hit: £495.'

Invisible fish

So how can you tell if someone is an expert? Sometimes we recognize experts immediately. We experience their work and can judge it for ourselves – in concert halls or theatres or exhibitions, or in work by people like Derek the taxidermist. Sometimes we trust in their expertise without seeing how they do it, as with surgeons, chefs or architects. Such experts seem mysterious, and most of us know we could never do their work ourselves.

Other experts are all around us, though we often fail to notice them. When we have our car fixed by a skilled mechanic, or a new bathroom installed by a master plumber, it's easy to miss how expert these people really are. Because cars and bathrooms are so familiar, we overlook the skill required to do a good job. We take this expertise for granted and hardly register it. Yet work of this kind is the fruit of decades of experience.

The perceived value of an expert's work has a lot to do with how we judge it, and this can be misleading. For many people, surgeons, airline pilots and concert pianists come fairly near the top, while garage mechanics, plasterers and plumbers come further down. Yet the essence of being expert – that wisdom that allows you to get to the heart of a problem and fix it with skill, judgement and care – cuts across these unhelpful hierarchies.

Part of the undervaluing of experts is because of familiarity – or its opposite. Taxidermy is so far outside most people's experience that Derek's expertise is plain to see. A plasterer skimming a ceiling or a carpenter making window frames may require an equal amount of artistry, craft and science to do a good job, yet because ceilings and window frames seem so ordinary we fail to recognize how expert these craftsmen are. In fact, the dexterity and precision of a surgeon and a joiner are surprisingly similar. They will both have walked a gruelling path. Yet the hierarchies that place surgery above joinery hide the common ground they share. The point about being expert is not the field you are in but what you have to do to get there.

Becoming expert, therefore, applies to us all. We each have our own interests and skills, whether driving or playing tennis, publishing or accountancy, using a computer keyboard or playing a musical instrument. But being expert is easier to recognize in others than in ourselves, whether you are composing emails or composing symphonies. Yet although experts often go unnoticed, we can spot them if we think to look.

It's like observing the natural world. One day I was walking along a riverbank with an old friend. He's a keen angler, and he was trying to explain his passion.

'It's not really about catching the fish,' he told me, 'it's about looking.' I didn't understand what he meant. When we reached a bend in the river, he pointed and said, 'There, do you see them?' I couldn't see anything special, just the water with a few leaves bobbing up and down and some flies swarming in the sunshine. 'Look, loads of them,' he said, and he told me the type of fish he'd spotted. I couldn't see a single one. 'Just relax and look a while, and you'll see them too,' he explained.

As I stood on the bank, I let my gaze soften. Gradually I realized that what I'd thought were surface shadows were in fact fish flitting underneath. I couldn't identify what kind, but I became aware that they were there. My friend had been fishing since he was a child. He could put together the tiny clues that told him what was happening. They formed a language that he could understand but I couldn't. Ripples in the water, fleeting shadows, the glint of the sun, the pattern of the flies darting above the surface. He knew how to interpret all of this and make sense of it, even telling one species of fish from another.

Experts are like these invisible fish – all around us but hiding in plain sight. Often they are so modest about their accomplishments that they hardly acknowledge them. In this book I will be like my friend was that day, pointing out the invisible fish that surround us and live within us. I'll describe how to recognize experts, explore the characteristics they share, and ask what we can learn for our own lives.

Researching experts is a challenge. They often struggle to explain what they do. Their work has become unconscious – inaccessible even to them, and almost impossible to put into words. But they can usually show you. When you visit them in their studio, workshop, performance space, clinic or operating theatre, you can watch them at work. Even then, it's difficult to grasp the subtlety of what they do, to understand the judgements they make and the wisdom they bring to their work.

You might wonder how to find experts whose work resonates with your own and whose experience can shed light on yours. If experts are invisible fish, how can you see them? One approach is to go where you know fish will be, to find a bend in the river where they congregate. One such place in the United Kingdom is the Art Workers' Guild.

I found the Guild quite by chance. I was wandering through Bloomsbury in central London some years ago and ended up in Queen Square. This site is well known in medical circles because of some famous hospitals, including Great Ormond Street Hospital for Children and the National Hospital for Neurology and Neurosurgery. My eye was caught by a beautifully painted sign over the door of No. 6 saying 'Art Workers' Guild'. It happened to be Open Garden Squares Weekend in London, when hundreds of organizations throw open their doors to passers-by. No. 6 Queen Square's was ajar. I stepped in and found myself in another world.

I discovered that the Art Workers' Guild was started

in 1884 by young designers and architects who wanted to bring the fine and applied arts together on equal terms. This was the time of the Arts and Crafts movement, and William Morris – the artist, textile designer, writer and social activist who was one of its leading figures – was an early Master of the Guild. Now the Guild includes experts in over sixty fields, from pottery to botanical illustration, portrait sculpture to architectural drawing, ornamental plasterwork to jewellery-making. In most groups of experts – a society of silversmiths, say, or glass blowers, or printers, or doctors – all members are from the same profession. The Art Workers' Guild is quite the opposite. Its membership is very broad, and many of the experts I'll introduce in this book are among them.

I became fascinated by these Art Workers. As individuals, they are all highly skilled – only those at the top of their field are invited to join the Guild. As a group, they share a belief in the importance of doing good work and also a quiet pride in having spent years mastering a difficult craft. All of them are unusual; many are downright eccentric. In the years that followed my first visit, I spent more and more time with them, and eventually I was invited to join the Guild myself.

Spending time with them and other experts – including the ones you'll meet in this book – gave me an insight into their work. I began to see parallels between their experiences and mine, even though none of them do anything connected with medicine. I was able to test out ideas about the path to becoming expert – ideas which evolved into the ones you'll encounter in this book. I've had the experience of walking down a path towards becoming expert in my life as a doctor, and I found this image resonated with others too.

The apprenticeship model

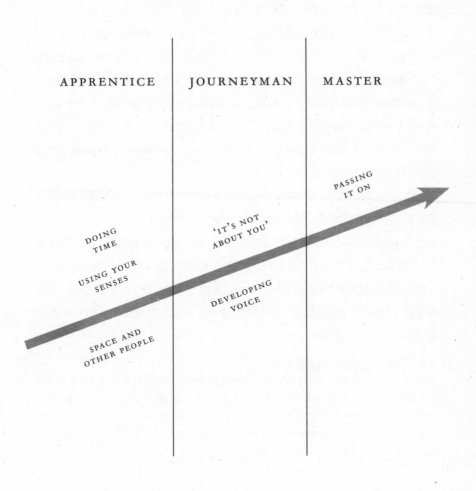

At the heart of this book is the apprenticeship model. This has been widespread throughout Europe for centuries and has counterparts all around the world. Many people associate it with the medieval guild system for becoming a craftsman (a long-established term, which now of course applies equally to men and women, and which for convenience I will use throughout this book). Although many apprenticeship systems in the UK are being eradicated by social, political and industrial change, the model remains useful for our thinking. Historically it has referred to learning a craft or a trade, but for me it applies to experts of every kind – from taxidermists to teachers, plumbers to pilots. It's a model that most people understand intuitively, even if they haven't thought about it in detail. Crucially, it captures the idea of progression. I'll use this model as a framework throughout this book.

Traditionally there are three phases – Apprentice, Journeyman and Master.* Of course, social conditions nowadays are radically different from those of medieval Europe. Apprentices no longer sleep behind the stove in their master's house or work for years without pay. But these stages provide a road map for anyone who wants to become expert.

---

* When I use these terms with an initial capital letter I'm referring to this common-sense use, without having to keep specifying that terms like 'journeyman' are nowadays gender-neutral. I'll use lower case for current usage, such as apprenticeship programmes in industry or when talking about mastery in other contexts.

1. **Apprentice.** You start by knowing nothing. You watch and copy others, learning to do things as they are already done in your master's workshop. Responsibility for your work and any mistakes you make lies with your master, and so does any credit for the work you do.

2. **Journeyman.** You launch your career as an independent expert. You leave your master's workshop and move around the country. Now you take responsibility for your own work, and you have to deal with the consequences of error. You continue to gain experience, refining and extending your skills and developing your individuality.

3. **Master.** Finally you set up a workshop of your own and teach others. You pass on your knowledge and expertise to future generations. You do what you can to look after the individuals who are learning from you; you have a sense of stewardship towards your field more widely; sometimes you even take the field itself in new directions.

These three phases are a useful way to think about the acquisition of skill. But they are descriptive, not explanatory. They identify points on a path, but they don't show you how to reach those points or how to know when you've got there. They divide the process into segments and treat these as if they were static. They measure what can be measured. But much that is important can't be measured. There are changes in who you are, not just what you can do. This process may be invisible from the outside. It's difficult to quantify, and may even go unnoticed from within.

Much research has focused on 'expertise', framing it in terms of impersonal attributes and capacities. Expertise is seen as separate from the person who acquires it. Expertise is being able to make a dovetail joint or put a basketball into the net. But I'm interested in what happens internally, in what it means to *become* expert, then become *an* expert, recognized by peers, the public and the outside world. I'm interested in what happens to that person when they learn to make a dovetail joint, rather than how they make the joint itself.

Descriptions seldom give an insider's point of view. They don't tell you what to expect if you want to become expert yourself, or where to place your effort. And they don't tell you how long it's likely to take, or the problems you'll encounter on the way. So I've broken down the Apprentice–Journeyman–Master model into smaller steps – the inside story of becoming expert. These steps form the chapters of the book. In the diagram on page 13 I've mapped them onto the Apprentice–Journeyman–Master framework. Of course, the steps don't always follow in an orderly sequence, and the stages often overlap. But they provide a sense of the terrain.

1. Apprentice

When you start out, your role is to learn. You're in some-one else's world, learning to do things their way, and they take responsibility for what you do. I've called this step **Doing time**. Your focus is on yourself – on the knowledge and skills you are acquiring. You are shielded from the impact of the mistakes you will inevitably make, both on the work itself and on you as a person. You become part of a community of practice, a group of people already doing what you aspire to learn. This community is usually supportive, though you may not experience it like that at the time. You are not expected, or even permitted, to depart from the established ways or try new things out. Your job is to conform, not to innov-ate. Your work involves repetition, boredom, trudging through menial tasks, and having to do things even when you don't understand why.

The next step – **Using your senses** – is about the fruits of doing time: the understanding you gradually develop of the work you are learning to do. You become familiar with the world you are starting to inhabit. You learn how it functions. You experience your work with your senses and your mind, as well as with your hands and your body. This applies whether you are becoming a stonemason or a doctor, attending evening classes in hat-making, learning the oboe as an adult beginner, or studying to become a lawyer, a film-maker, an account-ant or anything else.

The third step, **Space and other people**, is about being systematic with the materials and tools you work with – 'mise en place', as the chefs call it. At the same time, you develop sensitivity to the people you are working with: your colleagues or patients, customers or clients. You learn how to enter and work within other people's personal space.

By now you are getting ready to leave the Apprentice phase. Along with this comes **Getting it wrong and putting it right**. Mistakes happen, but so far you've been cushioned by being a novice. People expect you to get things wrong. Your environment is arranged so that you, your colleagues and your workplace are protected from the consequences of your errors. You start by working on material that doesn't matter, that can be replaced. You have people who will tell you when you're going off course and how to put things right. You're in a safe space. But in the next phase, that starts to change.

2. Journeyman

Now you're becoming independent – responsible for your work and how it's received. This transition from Apprentice to Journeyman entails two pivotal shifts. The first I've called '**It's not about you**', borrowing a phrase from magicians I've worked with. This requires a radical change in your focus of attention, shifting it away from yourself. Expert work involves doing something *for* someone else. Somewhere, there's an audience – a person or people who experience what you do – though you don't always see them directly. That audience may be obvious, as at a concert, a football match or a play. Here, expert and audience share space and time, and the work is synchronous. But in other fields, the audience is not there with you, and your work is asynchronous. When a potter makes a vase in a studio, there may be nobody else watching. But still the potter intends their work to be seen, whether in a shop, an exhibition or a display. Although the making takes place out of view, there is always an audience, even if theoretical, distant or completely unknown.

Whether you're an artist, a scientist, a clinician or a mechanic, this stage involves moving attention away from yourself. It's the shift 'from you to them'. 'Them' refers to the people who experience your work – your audience, patients or customers. This is a crucial transition, though it doesn't always happen at the same point on the path to becoming expert. Sometimes it doesn't happen at all. It's possible to be technically brilliant but remain focused on yourself; to miss or corrupt the heart of what you are doing. In my profession, the occasional rogue surgeons who carry out unnecessary operations, or experiment without their patients' consent, are often highly skilled. But they distort their work's purpose, coming to think it is more about them than their patients.

The second shift is **Developing voice**. I've taken this term from the world of jazz, where musicians will create a personalized musical fingerprint. As a performer, you reach a point where you are no longer a cog in someone else's machine, but a creator of expert work in your own right. As you establish your style, you develop your individuality. Now, you are shaping your work and giving it your signature. You are taking responsibility for being yourself and establishing your own identity. That requires confidence and self-belief. It's a subtle process, as it needs to develop in parallel with the transition to 'it's not about you' without making you arrogant or self-centred. You need to balance your emerging identity as an expert with a constant awareness of who your work is for. When this succeeds, you establish yourself as an individual, recognizable to those who experience your work.

Alongside these two shifts runs **Learning to improvise**. By now, you are taking responsibility for the successes and failures of your work, and you're responding to what life throws at you. You may be leading a surgical team, as I was. You may be developing your own research as a scientist, or setting up in business. You may be performing in public, writing a novel or heading up your department. Whatever your field, you'll be faced with the unexpected, and you'll have to improvise. When things go wrong, it's up to you to fix them. At the same time, as a Journeyman, you have freedom. You can develop new ideas, challenge existing methods, put your own stamp on the things you make or do. As we'll see, some of the most creative leaps come from serendipitous insights that nobody anticipated or planned. Improvisation is a hallmark of becoming expert.

3. Master

By this time you have become expert in the field you've spent so long studying. A few people go further, reimagining their field and taking it to a different place. In **Changing direction**, I examine what it means to reshape your field and take it in a new direction. Many of the experts in this book have done exactly that. One of these was John Wickham, a pivotal figure in the development of keyhole surgery.

In the final step, **Passing it on**, you are sharing your expertise with others and helping them grow. This requires another switch 'from you to them', but this time 'them' refers to people in your field: students, apprentices, and colleagues in your group or community of practice. Passing it on forces you to think about your own thinking. It makes you clarify what you do, distilling years of expertise into something you can share with others. Not all experts do this formally, establishing their own teaching practice or workshop. Not all experts do this at all.

This is when you take responsibility for supporting other people as they learn and for the errors they will inevitably make. You take the rap if things go wrong. You may 'pass it on' in other ways too. You might write a book or a blog, or share your work through television, radio or the internet. Whatever the format, passing it on is a marker of having become expert, a recognition that you have something worth sharing.

Being a Master is more than just conveying what you know. It is a relationship of care. You are as much a mentor and a coach as a teacher. You are taking responsibility for people who come along behind you, and you're contributing to your field. Often you develop a sense of stewardship, a concern for the sustainability of the work you believe in so strongly. Many experts join boards or teaching faculties, supporting groups of learners as well as individuals. The work of becoming expert is never over, but the Master always runs out of time.

This path to becoming expert makes things sound simpler than they are. Often, experts don't recognize or acknowledge that they have become expert, especially as there is no final point of completion. It's difficult to know when you've arrived. Or you may be expert in some areas but not in others.

Experts themselves are often the last people to recognize that they are expert at all. They might feel an imposter, constantly wondering when they're going to be found out. They are astonished that others want to come and learn from them. They may not feel they have achieved 'Master' status. But that doesn't mean they aren't expert. It just means that becoming an expert is different from having expertise. Often it takes someone else to recognize the distinction.

The journey from novice to expert is not linear. The stages are seldom as clear-cut as I've made them seem. The journey stops and starts and stutters. Often it feels like one step forward and two steps back. Becoming expert is about identity, about *becoming* a taxidermist, a tailor or a computer programmer; not just being able to do the things those people do.

This is a subtle but important distinction. It involves an ontological shift, a change in who you are as well as what you can do. This identity formation takes a long time and can be scary. Experiences along the way have profound effects: a serious error can forge a new resilience – or knock you back; extra responsibility can open up new horizons – or bring paralysing insecurity. All this builds into a cumulative experience that shapes what you become.

This book describes a path that runs from knowing nothing to passing on the wisdom of a lifetime. If you know it will take years to get there, you'll be less likely to give up after a few months if things aren't going well. There will be bumpy bits – long periods of boredom or frustration; bleak times when you don't seem to make any progress; points when you're tempted just to throw the whole thing over – and a map may help. Though a map won't keep you dry when it's raining, at least you're not lost.

You don't become an expert overnight. It takes a long time and a lot of effort. Without those, it won't happen. But how much time and how much effort? That's impossible to say, as it depends so much on each person. In the chapters that follow I will pull together the stories of people who have become experts, and try to make sense of their collective experience. Some of these stories are about the skills these experts had to develop, the way they learned to look and to do. Even more important are the shifts they made in their thinking and the self-awareness they gained along the way.

Being expert is hard to pin down. There's no clear moment when you 'get there'. You're in a perpetual state of becoming, zooming ahead in some areas and lagging behind in others. That's one of the things that characterizes true experts. They're always dissatisfied with where they've got to, always aware they could do things better.

Experts know that they can never stay still. It's like being in a boat, rowing slowly against the current. If you're not moving forward, you start to drift back. You can be proud of the work you've done, but you can never say that you have become as good as you will ever be. You have to keep moving, putting in energy, or you stagnate.

How this book is structured

This book is not about how to do the things experts do. That may be fascinating, but it's not my aim; I don't want to become a taxidermist, and I doubt you do either. Nor is it about expertise in abstract academic terms, though it does draw on what others have written.

Instead I lay down a challenge to move beyond the discipline-based thinking that keeps plumbers, neuroscientists, potters, magicians and heart surgeons in separate compartments. I highlight similarities and differences between experts, and I map a path from raw novice to wise mentor.

This book is about real people.

One of the strands running through the chapters that follow is my insider's perspective. That gives me access to things other people can't or won't say. I've drawn on my own experiences: the mistakes I've made, the thoughts I've had, and the ideas I've developed over the years. In my case, many of these are medical. That's inevitable, because I'm a doctor. My emphasis on clinical experiences is not because the world of medicine is unusually expert, but because that happens to be my story. If you were writing it, the central thread would be different. In that case you'd be drawing on other examples, making other connections. But the stages and themes would be similar.

In my professional career, I've changed direction several times and I'm still doing that now. I've been a surgeon, a family doctor, an academic and a university teacher, and in those areas I've become proficient. I have other interests too. As an amateur musician I'm still at the shallow end – nowhere near being an expert. And as a harpsichord-maker and a light-aircraft pilot I've had an initial taste, but never progressed beyond being a beginner. All of us do different things with our lives, and we're always at different staging posts along the path towards becoming expert. I've simply drawn on the parallels that are closest to hand for me, so I can draw comparisons.

At various points in the story, however, I'll bring in other strands and other experts. One of these is Joshua Byrne, a bespoke tailor I've been working with for over a decade. At first glance, Joshua's world and mine could hardly be further apart. After all, medicine is a science and tailoring is a craft – or so it seems. Yet our experiences have been surprisingly similar. We've been through the same stages, struggled with similar challenges. By comparing our experiences, our difficulties, and our ways of looking at the world, I will trace the shape of the path from Apprentice to Master.

I'll also bring in more people at the top of their game. I've already introduced Derek the taxidermist. Over the years I've had the privilege of meeting many others. Some are colleagues in medicine and science. Some are experts in the visual and performing arts. And there are pilots, magicians and craftspeople, too. I've watched them in their studios, workshops and laboratories, and I've spent hours talking to them. Those insights form the backbone of my research.

Though my own career has been medical, I'm not practising as a doctor now. If I'm expert in anything, it's education. When I work with students and trainee surgeons I see them struggling with the steps I've outlined.

I see them coping with boring repetitive work, developing skill in their hands and bodies, dealing with error, working with people, and going on to teach. I've also read what others have written about expertise, and tried to understand their theories and their ideas.

As you read this book another strand will emerge – your own. Everyone has their own experience of becoming expert, to a greater or lesser degree. Whether you're dedicating your life to a single focused aim or simply trying to get better at something you enjoy, the urge to become expert lies in each of us. It is difficult but not impossible. It's like running a marathon: anyone can do it if they train for long enough and persevere. Few of us will become world champions, but we can all try.

Experts under threat

So why is becoming expert important? In the book's final chapter I'll try to explain. For centuries, the apprenticeship system expected people to go through the lengthy process that leads in the end to mastery. Though becoming expert brings rewards, these rewards don't come instantly. There are no shortcuts, and immediate gratification is not on offer. This is increasingly at odds with our social world and its intolerance of doing things slowly. People are impatient, and they want to see results. They don't want to spend years in someone else's workshop before becoming independent.

In some ways, the work of individual experts is highly prized, especially in a world of uniformity and mass production. At the same time, experts as a group are being devalued and their skills dismissed. This is partly because the end result — a suit, a vase, a successful operation — conceals the work that has gone into it. The greater the expertise, the less you notice it. So it's often easy to imagine that you or anyone else could do the same.

But there's also a devaluing of expertise in society. Experts are seen as elite, unnecessary and dispensable, because information that was once their exclusive province can now be accessed at the click of a mouse. But this is a dangerous misconception. Information is not wisdom. And wisdom is what experts provide.

We have always needed experts, and I believe we always will. Partly that's because of what they can do for us: the services they provide, and the objects and experiences they create. But just as importantly, they give us inspiration. They show us what we can do if we really want to. At the end of this book I'll return to why experts are essential to us all and address questions I often hear, such as: Why should we seek to become expert in some areas of our life? Why are experts under threat? And what can we do about it?

I started this book with Derek the taxidermist posing his clouded leopard. But for now we'll leave Derek and go back several decades, to a hospital on the outskirts of Johannesburg in South Africa. I'm in the operating theatre with Simon, who has been disembowelled.

2. The surgeon and the tailor

It's 1981. I'm in Emergency Theatre B at Baragwanath Hospital and I'm about to start a trauma case. Baragwanath is in Soweto in South Africa – at that time one of the most violent places in the world. It's 4 a.m. on a Saturday night and Simon, a young Zulu man in his early twenties, has been stabbed. He's on a stretcher when I first meet him, coils of intestine spilling out of a wound in his abdomen onto the sheet that covers him. Night after night, patients like Simon are rushed into the 'surgical pit' for emergency treatment.

I've only been at Baragwanath for a short time, but already I'm used to seeing patients with their guts hanging out – evisceration, as the textbooks call it. I've learned that the dramatic-looking ones aren't always the most dangerous. But Simon* is really sick. He's not responding, he's slipping into unconsciousness and his blood pressure is dropping. He must be bleeding internally, and he needs immediate surgery.

We've rushed him to theatre. It's a busy intake, with several surgeons on duty. They are all in other theatres,

---

* I've changed names and other details of all the patients and clinical colleagues in this book, to preserve confidentiality.

29

dealing with their own cases. I'm in my twenties, eager to operate but still wet behind the ears. I've been a surgical registrar at Baragwanath for a year or so, and I've reached the stage where I should be able to do an operation like this on my own.

With elective (planned) surgery, you can start with 'easy' cases and build up. But with trauma surgery, you never know what you're going to find. Blades and bullets don't respect anatomy, and what starts off as a straightforward case can quickly turn into a nightmare. As I scrub up, I go through in my mind what I might encounter. I'm excited and terrified at the same time.

As soon as Simon is anaesthetized, I clean his skin, cover him with sterile drapes, then make an incision in his abdominal wall. I deepen it until I'm into the peritoneal cavity. Dark blood wells up and I can't see a thing. Lumps of maize floating on the blood and a sudden sour whiff of beer show there's contamination – the stab wound has gone into the stomach, at least. But my first priority is to stop the bleeding.

There's so much blood that at first I can't find where it's coming from. The temptation is to grab the first bleeding point I can see, but I force myself to slow down and be systematic, examining each of the organs in turn before deciding what to deal with first. Liver, stomach, small bowel, large bowel, spleen, pelvic organs. One by one I check them, sometimes by eye, sometimes reaching around corners to feel the parts I can't see.

I realize with a lurch that the stab wound is deeper

than I thought. It's gone down towards the head of the pancreas – tiger country for any surgeon, but especially one as inexperienced as I am. Blood keeps obliterating my field of view and I feel a rising panic. What if I can't cope, and my patient bleeds out on the table?

Becoming a surgeon

That night in the operating theatre with Simon I was certainly no expert, though I'd done a fair amount of surgery under supervision. I had started to do things on my own, to take responsibility for the decisions I made, but I hadn't had much experience in leading major operations. In terms of the path I outlined in the previous chapter, I was well into the Apprentice phase, and starting to become a Journeyman.

Fast-forward almost four decades. My career since then has taken me in unexpected directions. I'm not a trauma surgeon now. I'm not even seeing patients. Instead I've become a professor at a large London university, and I've specialized in surgical education. I spend a lot of my time exploring what it is to become an expert, and now I'm writing this book. It's a long way from where I began, and now I'll explain how I got here.

When I was starting that operation on Simon in Soweto in 1981, I'd been studying medicine for over ten years and was well into my training as a surgeon. The first six of those years were at medical school. Then my career kicked off in earnest. First came a year as a newly qualified house officer. Next I went back to the university where I'd qualified, and spent a year teaching anatomy to medical students. That was because I'd decided I wanted to become a surgeon, and I needed to pass the Primary Fellowship of the Royal College of Surgeons, a fearsome exam on anatomy, physiology and pathology. This was a stage on the way to gaining the Final Fellowship (FRCS for short), which was essential for becoming a consultant in the distant future. My anatomical knowledge as a medical student had been shaky to say the least, and I realized that the best way to learn was to teach.

After my time demonstrating anatomy, I'd been a junior doctor in orthopaedics, Accident and Emergency, and obstetrics. Then an opportunity came up to spend a year in South Africa. I leapt at the chance. Soon I found myself in alien and fascinating surroundings on the other side of the world. It proved so interesting that one year turned into two, then five. I completed my training as a specialist surgeon and became a consultant in South Africa.

For much of that time I worked at Baragwanath Hospital (now Chris Hani Baragwanath Hospital), or 'Bara' for short. Bara is in Soweto – South West Township, to give it its full name – on the outskirts of Johannesburg. At that time Soweto had a population of well over a million people. Bara was its only major hospital, and was one of the busiest in the world. This was towards the end of the apartheid era, and all the patients I looked after were black. They came from a bewildering array of cultures and spoke many languages. I'd never experienced anything like it.

Although we had patients with every kind of surgical condition, a lot of the time I was treating young men who had been stabbed or shot. Weekends were especially busy, as the migrant workers in Johannesburg would get drunk on payday and attack one another with pangas (machetes) or sometimes guns. It was gruelling, and I often worked for thirty-six hours at a stretch with no sleep. Of course, it wasn't all wounds caused by violence. Many of our older patients had horrible diseases like cancer of the oesophagus (gullet), which was especially prevalent in that part of Africa. We had our fair share of patients with perforated ulcers and strangulated hernias, conditions I was used to from the UK. I also encountered diseases I'd read about but never seen, like typhoid. A lot of the work was repetitive and routine. I spent hours in the 'septic theatre', draining the abscesses that were so common in our patients. But it was the trauma surgery I felt most attuned to.

Bara at weekends looked like a war zone, something I would experience for real a few years later. In Bara, as soon as the patients arrived they would be sorted by a process of triage. The most seriously injured were usually unconscious. Often nobody knew the patient's name, and they were recorded as something like 'Unknown Saturday Number x' until a friend or relative arrived to identify them. They would be put onto a trolley with a red 'URGENT' sticker on their forehead, covered with a grey blanket and wheeled into the aptly named surgical pit, where doctors and nurses would stabilize them. The surgical team on call would make an assessment, do an initial resuscitation and take any patient with life-threatening injuries straight to theatre for surgery. Simon was one of those.

In the operating theatre, Simon is bleeding profusely. I'm starting to panic. Fortunately, Sister Ramaphosa, my scrub nurse, is highly experienced. Just as well, as my first assistant this evening is a newly qualified doctor who doesn't like surgery. He usually stays out of theatre, where he's not much use. But at least he can hold a retractor, helping me to get a clear view inside Simon's abdominal cavity.

At last, my systematic exploration pays off and I find a severed artery pumping in the small bowel mesentery, a delicate stalk that supplies the small intestine with blood. Before I have time to think, Sister Ramaphosa has put a pair of artery forceps in my hand. I clamp the vessel, wait a moment, then breathe more easily as things start to come under control. Nobody has said a word.

It gives me time to explore more thoroughly. These stab wounds are treacherous, as you've no idea how long the blade was or where it went. Sometimes a small blood clot is the only clue to serious damage deep inside; that's why I have to be systematic. I mobilize the colon; it looks a bit suspicious, so I need to check behind it. I snip the filmy layer which tethers it to Simon's posterior abdominal wall, gently separating the anatomical layers. When I approach the duodenum and pancreas, I'm really scared. Repairing an injury here would take me way beyond my comfort zone. I look carefully, exploring millimetre by millimetre. Although there's bruising, none of the vital structures have been seriously damaged. It's a huge relief.

The next hour is filled with cutting and stitching: removing a section of small intestine, sewing the ends together again, closing the wound in the stomach. All things I'd read about in textbooks and seen a hundred times before but seldom done on my own. After a final check, I'm satisfied that I've repaired all the damage. I close Simon's abdomen with sutures, put on a dressing and take off the green drapes, now soaked with blood. My gown, too, is soaked, and I have to go and change before I can start the next operation.

Opening someone's abdominal cavity to see what's wrong inside is called a laparotomy. I'd learned the steps from my textbooks. But books don't tell you what it feels like to operate, or how to cope when you realize you're getting out of your depth. The people who write the books have experienced that, but when you're starting out, you haven't. You don't yet share a language with them. Even the sensation of cutting into a living human body is hard to describe. The slitheriness of living flesh, the feel of organs pulsating under your fingers, the click of the instruments as they lock into place – not to mention the hammering of your heart as you start a major operation, or the sick feeling in your stomach when things start to go wrong. Nothing you read in books or see on television can prepare you for the real thing.

And none of those textbooks ever described the physical pleasure of operating when it goes well or the fear when things go wrong. None of them mentioned the satisfaction of seeing a seriously ill patient that you've operated on walking out of hospital once they've recovered. Looking back, I can still feel that mixture of excitement and apprehension when I opened Simon's abdomen. I didn't know what I'd find. I didn't know whether I could cope. But once I'd started, I forgot my anxiety. It wasn't about me any longer; it was about Simon. I had to work out what his injuries were and do my best to fix them. I narrowed my focus and concentrated on each part of the procedure, as I'd been taught. Luckily things turned out well, but afterwards I'd replay it in my head, wondering if I could have done things better.

After that operation I realized I'd reached a watershed. I wasn't an expert by any means – far from it. I was still in the Apprentice phase. But I had managed to subdue my anxiety and perform a difficult operation that ended well. For the first time, I felt I was becoming *a surgeon*, rather than just somebody who was able to do a surgical procedure.

Later I discovered that this happens to experts in

many fields. Of course, when I was starting that operation I wasn't thinking of those other fields. I was a trainee surgeon, applying my scientific knowledge and physical skills to make an injured person better. It never occurred to me that I could learn from tailors, musicians, hairstylists or fighter pilots. Now, decades later, I wish I had.

Becoming a general practitioner

In the years that followed, operating on patients like Simon became routine. Some of the most urgent had been stabbed in the heart. We usually had several of these over a weekend, sometimes more. In the end, I became used to running at full tilt down the corridor to the operating theatre with a patient whose heart was on the verge of stopping. A few moments to transfer the patient onto the table, then making a skin incision, splitting the breastbone with a hammer and chisel, slitting open the pericardial sac and putting a stitch in a spurting ventricle. Once things were under control we could all take a breather while the patient's blood pressure came up and ours went down, before we started closing the chest.

After almost three years at Bara, I felt I was getting the hang of trauma surgery. I wanted to broaden my experience, so I moved to Cape Town. I'd decided to continue my training at Groote Schuur, the university hospital famous for the world's first heart transplant, performed by Christiaan Barnard in 1967. At Groote Schuur I was still treating a lot of trauma patients, but I also worked for some of the world's leading experts in liver disease, intestinal surgery, neurosurgery, paediatric surgery and intensive care. By rotating through these specialities I gained a broad experience which later proved invaluable. I took my FRCS exams, became a consultant, and for a few months headed up the paediatric trauma unit at Cape Town's children's hospital. Nominally independent, I was making the transition from Apprentice to Journeyman.

By then I had been in South Africa for more than five years, but I'd never intended to stay there. My parents lived in London and my mother had become seriously ill with cancer. It was time to go home. Before returning, though, I spent several months as a consultant surgeon in Oshakati, a small town in a remote part of Namibia and home to the Owambo people. I discovered when I got there that Oshakati was on the border with Angola, and at that time South Africa and Angola were at war. Although I'd seen a lot of trauma, I'd never worked in an actual war zone and I hadn't realized how dangerous it would be. I found myself catapulted into a world that was like nothing I'd ever experienced. In every sense, it was a baptism of fire.

Above all, it was lonely. In Cape Town there was always someone to ask if I got really stuck. In Oshakati, I was on my own. The hospital was huge, and the surgical section alone had more than two hundred beds. But it was chronically short-staffed, and the surgeon in charge when I arrived had been working without a break for more than three years. He had a suitcase in his hand when I got there – he left the same day and I never saw him again. I found myself responsible for the two hundred surgical patients, with only two junior doctors to help me.

In Oshakati, I had to grow up fast. As well as the patients already on the wards, new ones with serious injuries poured in every day. Most of the time I was way outside my comfort zone. Along with day-to-day surgical problems, like draining abscesses and dealing with appendicitis, I had to look after people who had been blown up by roadside explosive devices or hit by rockets, often suffering appalling injuries. I had to learn to improvise, performing operations I'd heard of but never seen – let alone done.

Some of the most horrifying injuries were from phosphorus grenades. The phosphorus would burn its way into the patient's skin and was almost impossible to remove. One of the Owambo theatre sisters showed me what to do. You give the patient a general anaesthetic, put them on the operating table, then turn out all the lights. You see which parts of the patient glow in the dark, then cut them away with a scalpel or root them out with a wire brush. It was nightmarish. No one had ever mentioned phosphorus grenades when I was a houseman in North Wales.

This is what I mean by saying that the path to

becoming expert isn't linear. In Oshakati, I was developing my voice as a Journeyman surgeon, but the demands of the work greatly outstripped my knowledge and confidence. I was taking responsibility for my decisions, and sometimes I got things wrong. Then my patients and I had to cope with the consequences.

When the time came for me to return to England I'd reached another watershed in my career. As a surgeon in Africa I'd spent a lot of time operating, then looking after my patients as they started to recover. But once they had been discharged from hospital, I never saw them again. I realized that, for me, there was something missing. I wanted to follow the stories of my patients over years, rather than days or weeks. And I wanted to experience other kinds of medicine.

One day while I was still in Cape Town, I had been leafing through the back pages of an out-of-date issue of the *British Medical Journal*. I spotted an advertisement for a one-year general practitioner (GP) trainee post in Lichfield, near Birmingham, in the English Midlands. The closing date had long passed, but I posted off an application anyway. A few weeks later, to my astonishment, they wrote back and offered me the position. So I ended up changing direction and retrained as a GP – a family doctor. It was a big step to take and my friends all thought I was mad. I knew it was a risk, but I thought it would be fascinating. And it was.

Changing from surgery to general practice was tough. I had to do a second apprenticeship. I learned a huge amount in my year as a GP trainee, though most of it wasn't new facts or techniques so much as new ways of putting my knowledge together. I wasn't quite back to square one, but I did have to learn a completely different kind of medicine.

When my year as a trainee was over, I started looking for a practice to join. Those were competitive times for GPs, and there were often more than 150 applicants for sought-after positions. I was lucky. I was offered a partnership with seven GPs in Trowbridge, a smallish town about a hundred miles from London. I was there for the next seventeen years, long enough to pass through several of the steps in this book. At first I was a greenhorn Journeyman, taking responsibility for my work but still with a great deal to learn. As my confidence grew, I developed my personal style as a GP. In time I began to pass my knowledge on, to teach and support other doctors as they in turn became expert.

As a GP, I developed a different way of applying the knowledge and skills I had acquired as a hospital specialist. I drew on my surgical training, but whereas in surgery you work with a patient very intensely over a relatively brief period of time, in general practice it's the opposite. You get to know your patients through repeated short encounters spread out over many years. I had the freedom to develop my own style – or what I describe in this book as 'voice'.

Becoming an academic

Once I was settled in my practice, I developed a teaching programme for GPs who wanted to carry out minor surgery. But when I tried to crystallize the surgical knowledge from my earlier career, I found it surprisingly difficult. I tried several approaches, including writing a textbook, but none of them really worked. I knew from my experience with surgical patients like Simon that books weren't always helpful, so in the end I developed a multimedia programme, working with a dermatology consultant (Julia Schofield), a recently formed simulation company (Limbs & Things) and an anatomical graphics company (Primal Pictures). We combined silicon models and computer graphics, so clinicians could practise surgical techniques at home.

Although I'd done a lot of teaching by then, I'd never studied education formally. I wanted to find out more, so I did a PhD at the nearby University of Bath. As I was studying, I linked my own experiences of teaching and learning to what people outside my field had written. I read their books, examined their theories, and tried to match them with my own ideas. That led to a third career change and took me to Imperial College London, the university where I now work.

At Imperial the wheel came full circle and I found myself with surgeons again. This time, though, I was teaching them about education rather than doing operations myself. I established a Master of Education (MEd) in Surgical Education, which for many years was the only one of its kind in the world. At the same time, I created simulations that integrated the physical skills of operating with the human skills of caring for sick people. I built a research group which has developed low-cost yet realistic recreations of surgery that can be carried in the back of a car and set up anywhere. Working with design engineers, we even developed an inflatable 'igloo', using lightweight props to recreate the sense of being in an operating theatre without requiring extensive equipment.

My first idea had been to use this portable simulation for training surgical teams. An epiphany came when I realized it could be used in a different way – to invite patients and members of the public to see what goes on inside an operating theatre and even take part in a simulated operation. We developed the idea of 'reciprocal illumination', a change in perspective for everyone who took part – surgeons, patients and the public.

These simulations enabled discussions with people who often felt excluded from the worlds of medicine and science. I became fascinated by public engagement, as it's called, and over the next few years this became the focus of my work. With the others in my group I put on literally hundreds of events at science festivals, museums, street fairs, public parks and music venues. In these events, I wasn't focusing on the details of anatomy and disease. Instead I was exploring the performance and craftsmanship of surgery. That led to what has become my main research – exploring points of connection with experts outside medicine.

Imperial College London is ideally placed for this. Within a few yards of the main university campus, in London's South Kensington, are some of the world's leading museums and institutions. These include the Science Museum, Victoria and Albert Museum, Natural History Museum, Royal College of Art and Royal College of Music. Not far away are the Art Workers' Guild, the City and Guilds of London Art School, the Royal Academy of Arts and the Wellcome Trust. Over the years I've developed connections with all of them.

Some of these connections have become more formal, such as the Royal College of Music and Imperial College London's Centre for Performance Science, which my RCM colleague Aaron Williamon and I established and jointly lead. In 2019, I became the Professor of Anatomy at the Royal Academy of Arts, a post first held by the famous anatomist William Hunter in 1769. Today, I work across many disciplinary boundaries to find out what it means to become expert.

The tailor

Now to Joshua Byrne, the bespoke tailor whose ideas have influenced me so profoundly. We've both travelled from Apprentice to Master and we've both had ups and downs along the way. Though our fields are completely different, our paths have been uncannily similar.

I met Joshua on a hot summer's day in 2009, when I was developing my third career, as an academic. His workshop is near Savile Row, the London street which has been the heartland of bespoke tailoring for centuries. When I first saw him, Joshua was stooped over a half-made jacket, with the Test match commentary on the radio in the background. Tall, bearded and impeccably dressed, Joshua has a warm, attractive personality. I'd never talked to a tailor before and he'd never talked to a surgeon. Tailors and surgeons don't normally have the chance to meet, and I didn't know what to expect. He seemed as curious as I was about the idea that we might have anything in common.

The first thing I noticed was Joshua's technical skill, and how it chimed with my own experience. When he described how he makes a suit, I was struck by the way we both use sewing. As an apprentice, Joshua spent years with a needle and thread, putting sleeves on jackets and shaping the layers of a suit. I did something similar during my years as a surgeon, joining intestines or blood vessels. As we talked, we discovered more common ground. It turned out that we had each been through two apprenticeships – one focusing on technical skill, the other more about people. We were each fascinated by the principles of our craft and the ideas that underpin it.

Halfway through his second year at university, studying agriculture and economics, Joshua by chance saw a film with a brief scene in a tailor's workshop. Suddenly, he realized that was what he wanted to do. There weren't any tailoring opportunities in Edinburgh at that time, so he left university and went to London to become an apprentice. Like Derek the taxidermist, Joshua had had an epiphany which changed the course of his career.

Joshua explained to me that there are two kinds of tailors. 'Making' (or 'sewing') tailors are the experts in construction. They build suits and jackets to the specifications of a 'cutting' tailor, who designs the garment and interacts with the customer. Both kinds of tailor are highly skilled, but their work is different and they inhabit separate worlds. An apprentice will usually choose one or the other, then stay on that side of the business throughout their career. But Joshua didn't do that; he trained in both. I had done something similar, changing from surgery to general practice. In doing two apprenticeships within the same world, we are both unusual within our fields.

I asked Joshua to give me a glimpse of a 'making' tailor's work. He showed me how he sews a sleeve onto a jacket. Watching him use a needle and thread with effortless grace took me back to my time as a surgeon, suturing stab wounds in Africa. So I asked him to let me try some sewing. Even though it had been over two decades since I last performed a major operation, I thought it would be pretty straightforward. After all, I'd had years of experience – how difficult could it be?

With a jacket on my lap, a needle in my hand and only

the window for a light, I found out. I felt completely use-less. I floundered, unable to do the simplest thing. I seemed to have lost all those sewing skills I'd spent years perfecting. It was horrible.

Thinking about it afterwards, I realized that despite the apparent similarities between our skills, our ways of working were completely different. I was used to operating in a team, standing up under a bright light in a surgical gown and latex gloves, with people handing me instruments and sutures when I needed them and taking them away when I'd finished. Every time I wanted to put in a stitch, an expert colleague like Sister Ramaphosa would pass me a curved needle mounted on a special instrument.

In Joshua's studio all that had gone. Tailors work alone. They use straight needles, holding them directly in their fingers rather than using instruments, and there's no one to hand things over or take them away. This made me question what I thought I knew about becoming expert. I realized my skill only made sense within its setting. Changing the context by visiting Joshua had brought that abruptly into view. Away from my team I felt adrift.

Though Joshua's work and mine are different, we'd had similar experiences as we travelled the path to becoming expert. As a beginner (an Apprentice) he had to do things without understanding why. He became skilled in the techniques of his trade and gained a deep understanding of the textiles and cloth he worked with. He'd had teachers who were inspiring and supportive, but also others who were critical and hostile. Later, as an independent craftsman (a Journeyman), he developed his voice – taking risks and striking out on his own. Now, as an expert (a Master), he was articulating that knowledge and passing it on. In my time as a junior doctor, a surgical trainee in South Africa, a consultant surgeon in Namibia, a GP in rural England and a university academic in London, I'd been through those stages too.

Since our first meeting, I've spent a lot of time with Joshua. At this point in our careers we're both trying to convey our knowledge to people less experienced than ourselves. Through our conversations, we've explored what it means to be expert, and every year Joshua takes part in the master's programme I lead at Imperial. This isn't just Joshua telling my students and me about tailoring; that's interesting, but not especially relevant to us as surgeons. It's also looking at how tailors become tailors, which makes us think about how surgeons become surgeons and why. As you read on, you might think about how surgeons becoming surgeons, tailors becoming tailors – or anybody becoming anything – shines a light on your own path, and why you're walking down it.

Looking outside your field

I've never become an expert quite like Derek the taxidermist and I know I never will. I've never spent forty-five years in one field. But I've developed what the sociologist

Harry Collins describes as 'interactional expertise' – the ability to speak the language of experts whose work you cannot do. Collins distinguishes this from 'contributory expertise' – the expertise of doing the work itself – which in my case is being a doctor and a teacher. Interactional expertise involves engaging with people outside your field. Most people have interactional expertise to some extent. Some, like journalists, make it their profession. Now it has become mine, too.

It's easy to imagine science, art and craft in watertight compartments. Yet we put ourselves in a straitjacket if we think of experts solely in terms of their occupation. Categories like medicine, tailoring or taxidermy emphasize difference, not similarity; we think of what makes these experts unique, not what they have in common. And we seldom find out how they got there, or how we can apply their knowledge to ourselves.

As Joshua and I have found out, there is a lot to learn from people outside your field. I'll never make a jacket and he'll never do an operation. But on a deeper level we understand one another's stories. We've both spent years learning something we believe in, and we've both had challenging times. We've struggled to gain physical skills. We've encountered difficult teachers, students, customers and patients. And we've looked beyond our field.

My conversations with Joshua and others have helped me talk my ideas into existence. Those conversations have been instrumental in shaping what I'm trying to say. As one of my patients once said to me, 'How do I know what I think until I hear myself tell you?'

Though Joshua's experience and mine don't coincide precisely, he sums up what being expert means to me. Joshua is driven by a passion to be the finest tailor he can be, and to do the best possible work for his customers and clients. That, to me, is the essence of mastery.

But I'm getting ahead of myself. Becoming expert is a long journey. At the start of this chapter I was in Emergency Theatre B at Bara in 1981, preparing to operate on Simon. My path had only just begun. I still remember that sick feeling as I wondered if I'd be able to cope with what I found inside his abdomen. Whatever your field, you'll have moments like that. The only solution is to build up experience, to do it over and over again. And that starts with doing time.

APPRENTICE | JOURNEYMAN | MASTER

PASSING
IT ON

DOING
TIME

'IT'S NOT
ABOUT YOU'

USING YOUR
SENSES

DEVELOPING
VOICE

SPACE AND
OTHER PEOPLE

3. Doing time

It's a Sunday in Manchester Royal Infirmary in 1974 and I've been sent to do 'the bloods'. For the whole morning I go from patient to patient, taking blood for routine preoperative tests. Nobody else wants to do this job, which is why I've been given it. It's the first time I've been in hospital as a medical student, and I'm feeling excited. Proudly wearing my new white coat, I've crammed my pockets with specimen tubes, syringes, needles and a wad of request forms. A harassed houseman (as newly quali-fied doctors were called at that time) showed me once what to do, then vanished, leaving me to face the ward on my own.

By now I'm halfway through my time at medical school. For three years I've been learning facts. I've spent hours in the dissecting room, memorizing anatomy. I've spent hours in the histology lab too, looking at slides under the microscope. I've learned about physiology, pharmacology and pathology. But I've never touched a patient.

My first two bloods are easy – patients with large juicy veins which are straightforward to puncture. My confi-dence blossoms, but not for long. It turns out I've had beginner's luck. Once reality kicks in, I discover that taking blood can be incredibly difficult. Some patients seem to have no veins at all, or thick hard ones like clay pipe stems, or deceptive ones that look easy but burst into huge bruises at the touch of a needle. Often I cause my patients pain as I try again and again. Although they're very understanding, I feel dreadful.

Even managing the kit is a challenge. I need at least four hands to hold the syringes, needles, tourniquets, sticking plasters and swabs. In spite of all the facts I've learned, when it comes to doing, I'm all thumbs. Just as bad are the triplicate forms, and the specimen tubes with tiny shiny labels which my biro won't write on properly. Yet unless I'm meticulous, the forms and tubes can get muddled up. That could be disastrous.

Quite apart from the physical skills of blood-taking, I have to develop ways of keeping track, ensuring I can put my hand on things when I need them. Nobody told me about that part. I've had to create a system for myself. It's tough, but gradually I get the hang of it, and after a few more Sundays I feel a lot more confident. A couple of months later, that new confidence takes another hit.

I've been sent to insert a cannula ('put up a drip', as it's often called) in a patient who's been admitted on the emergency 'take'. His blood pressure is low, the house-man is busy and I've been told to set up an intravenous infusion. I've seen it done, and it looked straightforward enough. After all, I've learned how to take blood now, so I should be able to put a cannula into a patient's vein. Then reality kicks in. Faced with a sick patient, a bag of sterile saline and yards of plastic tubing, I have no idea what to do. I'm back to square one.

The value of repetitive work

If you've struggled to get the hang of something new, you'll be familiar with this frustration. It goes with the territory of being an Apprentice. Joshua the tailor experienced something similar when he started learning to be a jacket-maker. At that stage he wasn't designing three-piece suits, any more than I was performing operations. He was in a workshop in the house of his master, Ron, making pocket flaps. He made hundreds of them, and they drove him round the bend.

Pocket flaps aren't as simple as they sound. They have to be cut with great precision so they fit the subtle curve of a jacket and don't gape when it moves. They have to be sewn with accuracy and they must look perfect. But making them is repetitive and tedious. Ron had an exacting nature and insisted on the highest standards in his workshop, but he wasn't a natural teacher. Every so often he would look at Joshua's work, then shake his head and say, 'No.' No explanation, just 'No'. He wasn't satisfied, but he never said why. So Joshua had to keep on making more pocket flaps. He almost went out of his mind with boredom.

Sometimes, like me with the bloods, Joshua would have beginner's luck. He'd make a pocket flap that Ron was happy with. But that was just a fluke, and Joshua couldn't recreate it. For a long time, he couldn't tell how he was doing. But gradually he began to recognize when his own workmanship was good and when it was still flawed. All that repetition meant that Joshua became able to set the standards for his work and develop consistency. At last Ron was satisfied and allowed him to move on to other tasks, though to this day, when Joshua thinks of pocket flaps he thinks of boring repetitive tasks of no apparent value. Yet, as we'll see, the pocket flaps of this world do have value. Without that experience, Joshua would never have become the master tailor he is today. Likewise, without doing the bloods, I'd never have become a surgeon. There's an equivalent in every field.

Of course, it wasn't just pocket flaps. All through those years as an apprentice, Joshua was doing many kinds of repetitive work. After pocket flaps came making buttonholes, stitching edges, 'felling' linings, inserting padding and shaping lapels. Later he was entrusted with more difficult tasks, like putting in sleeves, collars and under-canvas. But each task required repetition, and it soon became tedious.

I went through something similar as my career developed. Being a medical student was frustrating enough, but once I qualified things got a lot worse. A large part of my work when I became a houseman involved taking more blood, unblocking urinary catheters and siting intravenous drips – usually in the middle of a night on call, when I'd just got back to sleep. Boring, repetitive tasks. Important to the patient, of course, but of no apparent value to me. In time I became adept at doing these tasks, but I couldn't see why it needed six years at medical school to stick needles into people's veins. Why couldn't someone else do it?

But this was the first step on my path to becoming expert. Here, you're so inexperienced that you don't even know what you don't know. You can't see the bigger picture. Your fingers are all thumbs. Often you're scared and bored at the same time. You're thinking about yourself.

All the experts I've talked to told me a similar story.

Paul Jakeman is now one of the country's leading historic stone carvers. Soon after I met him, he showed me the massive stone unicorn he carved for the steeple of St George's, Bloomsbury, in central London. Weighing several tons, it replaces the original in what is one of Nicholas Hawksmoor's iconic churches. But Paul hasn't always been carving unicorns. When he started his stone-carving apprenticeship several decades ago, he had no idea what to expect.

He'd imagined himself on a high ladder, restoring medieval statues in an English cathedral. But instead he spent weeks sweeping up stone dust in the mason's yard and making the tea. The first task his master set him was to create a perfectly flat horizontal surface in a block of stone, using only a chisel and a dummy (a mason's mallet). As the months went past and his block of stone grew smaller, he almost went out of his mind with boredom. Finally he showed his work to his master, who declared himself satisfied. At last, Paul thought, the real work would begin. But he spent the next six months with another block of stone, this time creating a perfectly flat *vertical* surface. He almost went out of his mind with boredom – again. But it wasn't until he'd mastered those basics that he was ready to go near anything that mattered.

So how can you make sense of this repetitive work? As you struggle with pocket flaps, or bloods, or vertical stone surfaces during your first apprenticeship, you discover something important. As Joshua put it to me: you can allow yourself to go out of your mind with frustration, switching off your brain and letting your mind wander as you endure the tedium. Or you can do something about it.

The secret to coping with boredom is to focus on doing each task as well as you possibly can – whatever that task is. It may sound obvious, but it's up to you to decide whether you find something boring, and you can change that if you choose. By paying close attention to tedious work, you reframe it. Instead of being a waste of time, it becomes a means of moving forward. You shift your focus from the frustration of the task to the skills you are gaining by doing it. Joshua told me that he came to see pocket flaps as an opportunity to hone his skills. The expert sewing he showed when

I first met him would never have developed without that repetition.

By deciding to be 'present' in his work and concentrate on it fully, Joshua made rapid progress. He became familiar with his materials. He reframed that never-ending pile of pocket flaps as a series of opportunities to improve and develop. If he had been listening to the radio or chatting to a friend while he worked, he wouldn't have been paying attention. He might have learned how to do the tasks, but he would never have found out why he was doing them. He wouldn't have progressed. Paul the stone carver had a similar experience. By gritting his teeth and perfecting those horizontal and vertical surfaces, he laid the foundations for the effortless skill he eventually developed.

The reality is that in any job there's a lot that's tedious, but it just has to be done. Nobody is entitled not to be bored. Unless you find ways of accepting that, you're likely to have a hard time. Yet in our climate of immediate gratification and continual stimulation, coping with tasks that are inherently boring is becoming a lost art. We tend to think that tedious tasks should be hived off, to technology or to other people. But this is missing the point. The boring bits are part of the work. Bypass them and you lose something essential.

For many experts, the boring parts remain central to what they do throughout their career. Andrew Garlick has been making harpsichords for over forty-five years, and his instruments are in demand all over the world.

His signature instrument is a double-manual harpsichord, based on a 1749 French masterpiece by Goujon that is today housed in a Parisian museum.

Andrew makes every part of each harpsichord himself. From shaping the soundboard and cutting out the keys, to stringing the instrument and painting the case, he does it all by hand. It's very labour-intensive, and he can only make five harpsichords a year. I asked him if he had help for doing the boring bits, and he said no. For him, the boring bits are part of the satisfaction of making a whole instrument, of knowing that he has created everything from start to finish. Although cutting all those keys is a tedious task that somebody else could do, Andrew recognizes that it's part of doing 'good work'. Boring or not, he has reframed it as worthwhile. The tedious tasks are part of being responsible for the work he does. That responsibility is part of becoming expert.

Learning to work in a team

In this early stage in our apprenticeships, Joshua, Paul and I were working in someone else's territory, on their terms. We had little agency. It was the same after I qualified as a doctor and started to specialize. Early on I knew I wanted to become a surgeon, so I took every opportunity to be in the operating theatre. What I really wanted was to do operations myself, but instead I was only allowed to 'assist'. This involved holding on to retractors to keep organs out of the way, so that the chief surgeon could get a good view.

I spent hours clutching the handle of a curved metal instrument whose other end was out of sight, being yelled at by the surgeon when I let it slip. I was at the bottom of the heap, and in a big operation with several assistants there were times when I couldn't see anything at all. Nobody gives a damn about the comfort of the third assistant, and I often ended up grappling with boredom and backache at the same time. I could see why American surgical residents described retractors as 'idiot sticks', because even an idiot could hold one. It seemed a complete waste of time. Why couldn't someone else do it?

Having been the lead surgeon in countless operations since, I now realize how important it is for everyone to focus on their part. I know how exasperating it can be when a member of your team stops concentrating. You're about to clip and tie a bleeding artery, when a loop of intestine slips out from behind the retractor your assistant is supposed to be holding. The artery disappears from view and you have to start all over again. It's infuriating. For the bored assistant, it's just another example of them not yet understanding the bigger picture – of not recognizing the value of essential, albeit dull, work.

When I started my surgical training at Baragwanath Hospital in Soweto, I had to take my turn draining abscesses in the septic theatre. These were the cases more experienced surgeons didn't want to do. There's little glamour in pus, and I was left to carry out these smelly procedures on my own. Of course, I knew abscesses were horrible for the patients who had them, and I tried to do these procedures as well as I could, but at the time I didn't find them very interesting.

Later, I experienced something similar as a GP trainee. One of my jobs was to see the 'extras' – the patients who turned up after the morning or evening session had finished and needed to be squeezed in. Mostly they had straightforward problems: children with earache, women wanting the morning-after pill, or people whose repeat prescription had run out. To me at the time, this part of the work seemed almost trivial. But it wasn't trivial at all, and I was learning far more than I realized. The starting point for any expert is to spend time – lots of time – in the world you'll be joining. You have to become familiar with the materials, tools and people who make up that world. It's often tedious and dispiriting, but unless you put in that time, you won't leave the starting blocks.

Of course, you don't start entirely from scratch when you become an Apprentice; the path to becoming expert begins way back, in early childhood. Long before I was studying anatomy, let alone doing the bloods on a hospital ward, I was gathering relevant knowledge and skills. At home and at primary school I learned how to read, to write and to make. I tried out lots of things and got them wrong. At secondary school the process continued: I absorbed more facts, I did more with my hands. I learned the rudiments of science, of what to do in a laboratory. And, like everyone else, I worked with people. I learned how to get along with the children in my class, including the ones I didn't like and who didn't like me. It's the same for all the experts in this book and any of you reading it. Joshua the tailor and Paul the stone carver had both been working with their hands for decades before they started their chosen careers, and they'd been working with other people.

In order to join any group, you have to earn your place. As we've seen, this usually starts off by doing the jobs that nobody else wants. Often, these tasks act as a rite of passage, an initiation. When you're learning martial arts in Japan, you start by cleaning the sensei's rice bowl. When you're making pocket flaps, or taking blood samples for the coming week's operating list, you're showing your willingness to be part of the work as a whole, not just cherry-picking the bits you find interesting.

When you start, you're at the bottom of the pile. You get the jobs nobody else wants. You can't see how your tasks fit with what other people are doing. The work is often irksome and you have to do what you're told. Nobody cares whether you like it or not, and you feel like a cog in a machine. When I started as a houseman, a doctor who had been in the team a year longer than I had took me to one side and explained how things worked. 'It's simple really, Roger,' he said. 'Shit flows downhill and you're at the bottom.'

Communities of practice

One important outcome of this frustrating work is that you get good at skills you'll need later on. Like it or not, you have to be able to take blood or make pocket flaps. But another aspect is that you join a community of practice.

The idea of communities of practice was developed by Jean Lave, a social anthropologist, and Etienne Wenger, a teacher with an interest in artificial intelligence. According to their thinking, we are all members of multiple communities. When we join a football club, change our job, learn a new skill or go into a different class at school, we are becoming part of a new community. Each community is made up of concentric circles, and we start on the periphery. But even when we're on the edge we are 'legitimate participants' and we have the right to be there. We've joined the football club, so we're different to somebody who is thinking about joining the football club. But even though we've made a start, we can't do much yet. There's a lot to learn before we become a member of the team.

Learning on the job can be scary. Sometimes people show you what to do and how the system works, but often they don't. They just expect you to know. But how can you?

Soon after my experience with the bloods, I went into the operating theatre for the first time. A kindly houseman in the changing room showed me how to find scrubs and boots of about the right size, how to put on a cap and mask, and which theatre to go into. Feeling very professional, I went through the doors to where an operation was in full swing. Suddenly someone screamed 'DON'T DO THAT!' and everyone turned to stare at me. I wanted to fall through a hole in the floor. To this day I've no idea what I did wrong. All I know is that I broke some rule I didn't even know existed.

So how can we make sense of something like that when it happens? As a newcomer, a lot of what goes on in a community seems incomprehensible. Gradually the newness wears off and we get to know people, we watch how things work, we find out how people 'do things around here'. It's a slow process, but all that time we are learning from others in the group. The junior doctor who told me 'shit flows downhill and you're at the bottom' was only slightly more experienced than me, but he had learned something I hadn't. He had become part of the community I was only starting to join. He had an insider's understanding of how it really worked, and he let me into a secret the books had never told me.

As you spend time in a community, you move towards its centre. Lave and Wenger's term for this is 'legitimate peripheral participation'. It's a clunky phrase, but it captures the process of moving to and fro. They use it to speak 'about the relations between newcomers and old-timers, and about activities, identities, artifacts, and communities of knowledge and practice'.

Communities have fluid boundaries, and relationships between colleagues shift and re-form. When I was
taking blood and re-siting drips in the middle of the night,
I was at the centre of a community of junior doctors.
But when I presented the patients to my consultant on
the ward round the next day, the landscape had shifted.
She was at the centre and I had moved back towards the
edge.

In any group, you gradually become more confident,
moving steadily inwards. But whenever you join a new
community of practice, you start all over again. Things
which have become second nature as a central participant in one community may no longer hold when you
are peripheral in another. This happened to me every
time I moved up a stage in the surgical hierarchy, from
being a houseman to a registrar, then from registrar to
consultant. Every time you progress to another level,
you have to do an equivalent of taking bloods or making
pocket flaps. Whatever your area of interest, you'll have
your own experience of moving across boundaries.

By doing time, Joshua the tailor, Paul the stone carver
and I were each forming a bedrock of essential knowledge without realizing it. This knowledge isn't just
theoretical. It's the knowledge of 'doing': the physicality
of materials and bodies. It doesn't come from books and
you have to experience it for yourself, stocking an internal
library of sensations, muscular actions and familiarity
with your materials – *especially* when those materials are
other people.

Working with people

Some experts spend most of their time with other people. Hairstylists are a good example. Fabrice Ringuet has over thirty years' experience as a stylist and a teacher. He has been director of training at the Toni & Guy Academy and now runs masterclasses. He has spent years distilling his knowledge and skills as he trains apprentice hairstylists. For Fabrice, like me, doing time started with the jobs no one else wanted, such as sweeping the floor between customers or making tea for the clients as they waited. It was boring, frustrating work which stopped him from doing what he really wanted – to cut, to style, to be creative.

Gradually, Fabrice began to work directly with customers. After doing menial tasks for a long time, he progressed to washing clients' hair. In the process, he learned what hair looked and felt like – long hair, short hair, straight and curly, old and young. At the same time, he learned about people, and about himself. He learned to overcome his shyness, gently massaging each client's scalp as he applied the shampoo.

But when he started washing hair, Fabrice would get things wrong. Like all trainee stylists, he'd sometimes get soap in a client's eyes. He had to apologize, put things right and retain their confidence in the salon. Like me with the bloods, Fabrice was relating to people. He studied how to approach clients as they were sitting in a chair and watching him in the mirror. He learned how to enter their personal space without making them feel uncomfortable. Eventually, though, he progressed to cutting a straight edge in long hair. Though it was a seemingly simple task, it pushed him to a new level, and once again he discovered how difficult his craft could be.

During those endless hours of sweeping up and shampooing, then cutting straight edges in long hair, Fabrice was laying the foundations of his later expertise. As he developed his skills, he was moving towards the centre of a community of practice. He would draw on this experience later in his career, when he took responsibility for teaching other stylists.

This kind of knowledge can't be rushed or short-circuited. You have to build it up through experience, and it sets its own pace. Like making a cake, you can't finish it in half the time by baking it at twice the temperature. Learning to 'do' is not like cramming facts for an exam and forgetting it all a week later. The process takes time and has to ripen.

This bodily awareness is like a language learned through constant practice. How much pressure to apply, when to back off or take a break, and when to call for help – all these kinds of knowing evolve at their own speed and cannot be forced. Once mastered, however, the slow knowing pays dividends. Those cumbersome steps and unfamiliar movements become automatic, an unconscious part of what you do. Eventually, you stop thinking about component skills and focus instead on the outcome.

All of us learned our skills by doing tedious things again and again. Joshua's sewing needle became an extension of his hands, and in the end he didn't have to think about it. I could get blood from almost anyone with my syringe and needle, even when I was half asleep. Paul Jakeman could make a flat stone surface on autopilot, and Fabrice could cut someone's long hair in a straight line while chatting to them about their holiday. Eventually, we no longer relied on beginner's luck. We could make our materials do what we wanted every time. To get to that stage, though, we had to become comfortable with our materials.

To a non-specialist, it may seem that cloth is just cloth and stone is just stone. Human bodies, too, seem roughly similar. And at first glance you might think that hair is just hair. But this isn't the case at all. Cutting a straight line in two different types of long hair is a different physical experience.

It's the same with all materials. Every length of cloth, every piece of stone and every person is infinitely varied. It is impossible to learn a technique in the abstract. Skills only make sense in the context of *that* length of cloth, *that* piece of granite, *that* unique human being.

So far I've talked about the physical world. But 'materials' don't have to be something you can touch or see. If you're working with words, with stocks and shares, or with computer code, you are engaging with the materials of your work. Learning to handle these intangibles takes just as much time as working with their physical counterparts. You still have to spend time grappling with the basics, then learning how to shape and mould them.

Minimizing surprise

Certainly the skills which Joshua and I and the others mastered are useful in their own right. Jackets need pocket flaps and patients need blood taken. These tasks may not be interesting to the person doing them, but they have to be done. But there's more. By doing that repetitive work, we not only spent time with our materials and our tools, we became part of multiple systems. The first is the community of practice I described earlier. The second is the physical system by which any workplace is structured and set out, which I'll examine in the next chapter. The third is the internal system within our heads which we populate by repetition. This can be explained by a neuroscientific concept called 'predictive coding'.

The idea here is that the brain's job is not to absorb and process everything. Instead, it is meant to minimize surprise. The more you've experienced, the less surprised you'll be. This is particularly true of things that look roughly the same. For instance, each piece of cloth you work with might be different, but making a pocket flap to a specification minimizes variation. That makes life easier. As I got the hang of the bloods, I started to recognize patterns – to spot which veins were like clay pipe stems, and which ones would burst into huge bruises at the touch of a needle. I became aware of a landscape of common variations, and I adapted my technique accordingly. Like a beginner at chess or bridge, I came to realize that the number of common opening gambits is relatively small. Once I knew them, I could often see trouble coming before it arrived. That's predictive coding.

As we develop, our brains assemble a series of 'probability priors' – predictions of what is likely to happen next. If the outcomes happen as anticipated, the brain doesn't do much. It just recognizes that things are as it expected. But if the anticipated outcomes *don't* happen, the brain registers surprise and takes appropriate action. Our prior knowledge sets hypotheses and tells us what's likely to happen. Our senses provide confirming or disconfirming evidence.

The difference between experts and non-experts in a field is that the experts have built up a rich set of expectations based on their previous experience, so they can 'sample for difference'. That stops them having to waste energy in processing everything they encounter. Non-experts, on the other hand, have to start from scratch, analysing and interpreting information from all their senses.

This helps to explain the value of doing time – the gradual exposure to a range of experiences and sensory impressions that prime the brain with a knowledge of what to expect. That kind of knowing takes a long time to gain, but once embedded it is seldom lost. The traditional example is riding a bicycle. Those early experiences of interacting with the physical world – balance, coordination, the sensation of gravity – allow us to get on an unfamiliar bicycle years after we first learned, and ride without falling off. Even when verbal memory unravels, this physical memory often persists. And it applies to the world of surgery too.

I discovered this a couple of years ago when I was talking to Mrs Florence Thomas. When we met, she was ninety-seven and had just gone into a nursing home. I was doing some research into the history of surgical operations in the twentieth century, and I was keen to talk to Florence because I knew she had been a senior scrub nurse in a London teaching hospital during the Second World War. I wanted to ask her what that was like.

Florence had helped to run the operating theatres during the Blitz. Later in the war, she met a serviceman and they decided to get married. At that time, nursing was for unmarried women only. You could be a nurse or you could be married, but not both. So Florence left her profession, married the serviceman, had a family and never had anything more to do with healthcare. When I met her some seventy years later, her memory was very poor. She had difficulty recollecting anything about those days, or putting her experiences into words. At first I thought we weren't going to have much of a conversation.

By chance, though, I had a surgical instrument in my

briefcase and I gave it to her. Turning it over in her hands, she began moving its tip in a circle as if putting in a suture. Then, to my astonishment, she told me its technical name. 'These were called artery forceps, as far as I remember,' she said. When I asked her how she would pass that instrument to a surgeon, she turned it round and slapped the handle down in the unmistakeable manner of an experienced theatre nurse. Even when her words had failed, her body still remembered. The feel of that instrument reactivated her physical memory.

Models of expertise

So how do people become expert? A lot has been written on the subject and many researchers have come up with conceptual models. A well-known one maps out four stages. It looks like this:

1. *Unconscious incompetence* is when you don't even know you can't do it.
2. *Conscious incompetence* is when you're painfully aware that you aren't much good.
3. *Conscious competence* is where you can do it if you concentrate, but you have to think about what you're doing.
4. *Unconscious competence* is the final stage, the effortless mastery of the true expert.

This makes sense when you think about learning to

drive. You move from those initial lessons – when you can't coordinate the clutch with the gear lever, or turn the wheel and look in the mirror at the same time – to when you arrive home after a two-hour journey whose details you can't remember, because you were absorbed in a conversation with your passenger. The doing has become automatic, and the driving looks after itself. But how?

An influential figure in researching expertise is K. Anders Ericsson, whose lifelong work has become popularized by other writers such as Malcolm Gladwell. For decades, Ericsson has been studying 'elite performers' in music, chess and other fields, trying to work out their secret. His research shows that all successful experts have put in at least ten years – or ten thousand hours – of practice. This magic figure has even become a mantra, enshrined in popular culture. But Ericsson's work is often misinterpreted as suggesting that anyone who has put in that amount of practice will inevitably become an expert. In fact, Ericsson is saying that nobody becomes an expert *without* having done their time – not that putting in ten thousand hours will guarantee success. There's more to becoming expert than just practice. If Joshua hadn't spent all that time making pocket flaps, he wouldn't be the master tailor he is today. But if he hadn't made sure to build on that skill and develop further, he would just be good at making pocket flaps. Now his work has gone far beyond the technical proficiency that repetition brings.

One of Ericsson's insights has been into the nature of

practice. Many people reach what he calls a 'stable performance asymptote' – good enough to do what they want, but without pushing themselves to become exceptional. This applies to anyone learning club-level tennis, for example, or driving a car. But if you want to become an expert, Ericsson says, it's no good just doing the same thing over and over again. Practice must be sustained, deliberate, supported by expert feedback, and carried out with the intention to improve. Otherwise it's just a job or a recreation.

Other writers see things differently. I especially like the concept of routine and adaptive expertise, developed by the educational researchers Carl Bereiter and Marlene Scardamalia. Routine expertise is when you learn to do something in a particular way, then do it that way each time. For repetitive tasks like taking blood, making pocket flaps or creating harpsichord keyboards, this works well. You don't want to invent a new technique every time you do a simple task, or spend unnecessary brainpower on repetitive work. Instead you become good at doing things in a specific way and can hand that task over to your internal autopilot. In the example of learning to drive, this is effective for dealing with predictable situations. The difficulty comes when something unexpected arises, because then you need to think differently. As the psychologist Abraham Maslow is credited with observing, 'it is tempting, if the only tool you have is a hammer, to treat everything as if it were a nail'. You interpret new problems in the light of pre-existing solutions. And that can lead to bad decisions.

Adaptive expertise, on the other hand, is about being able to come up with new approaches. People who develop adaptive expertise deliberately seek new challenges, putting themselves into uncomfortable positions that force them to think afresh. Becoming good at something that used to require effort frees up your mind, and adaptive experts use this spare capacity to improve their skills. Bereiter and Scardamalia describe this as 're-investing freed-up attentional resources into progressive problem-solving'.

Returning to the driving example, instead of using that extra attentional capacity to talk with their passenger or listen to the radio, an adaptive expert might invest it in developing advanced driving techniques – reading the road more skilfully, driving in the fog, or practising in skid pans. I think we all have the capacity to develop both kinds of expertise, and to switch between routine and adaptive modes. When we do, the results can be life-changing. Or in Juan Manuel Fangio's case, life-saving.

It was 1950, and Fangio – one of the world's best racing drivers – was taking part in the Monaco Grand Prix. When a multi-car pile-up happened early in the race, Fangio was in the lead, one lap ahead and driving at top speed. The crash site was ahead of him but out of view, beyond the next corner. A fatal smash seemed inevitable. But instead of careering into the pile-up,

Fangio suddenly slowed down and stopped just before he reached the wreckage. Asked about it later, he explained that in preparing for the race he had been looking at a photograph of a similar accident in 1936. When he came out of the chicane towards the pile-up, he was aware that the crowd looked somehow different – a different colour. He realized that they weren't looking at him but were facing in the other direction, and he was seeing the backs of their heads. Something ahead of him was interesting the crowd more than seeing Fangio coming towards them. He remembered seeing something similar in the photograph, braked hard, and stopped just short of the crash.

This must all have happened in a fraction of a second, when most drivers would have been using all their attentional resource to stay on the track at such blistering speed. But in that moment, Fangio was able to notice that something was wrong, process that information, and make sense of what he saw – all with time to do something about it. Afterwards, the laconic Fangio just said: 'I was lucky.' But to me that isn't luck, it's adaptive expertise.

All this raises questions about the importance of doing time, and the experience of people like Joshua, Fabrice or me when we were starting out in our careers. From our perspective, we were just doing what we had to do, not engaging in sustained deliberate practice with the specific intention to improve, as Ericsson puts it.

Our work was dictated by the environment we were in and the expectations of the people we were with. Nobody cared about our feelings or what we were learning. Yet whether we were aware of it or not, prolonged immersion in the work we had chosen allowed us to stock up an internal library of 'doing' – a store of bodily knowledge that no amount of book-learning could have provided.

In the case of clinical medicine, book knowledge and 'doing' are often out of sync. When I teach medical students how to take blood or suture a wound, they are often astonished at how troublesome they find it. High achievers throughout school and university, they are accustomed to mastering new knowledge without difficulty. But then they encounter these apparently simple physical tasks that lie outside their experience. That makes them feel like a five-year-old struggling to tie their shoelaces, and it comes as a shock. Unlike Joshua the tailor or Paul the stone carver, these students have not been working with materials and tools since day one. They lack the confidence that comes through continual exposure.

Knowing that it will take a long time to grasp such skills is helpful when we come to learn something new. It shows that doing time can't be bypassed. It shows that some skills can be unexpectedly elusive, taking much longer to master than you expect. And it shows why you sometimes get stuck.

The intention to improve

When I was a GP, I learned to juggle. For several months, I went to lessons in a civic hall near my practice. Adrian, the teacher, was an inspiration. Tall, gangly and covered in tattoos, Adrian was one of the best performers in the UK, known at juggling conventions across the country for his superstar command of seven- and nine-ball patterns.

I started juggling with three balls. Learning this most basic of forms takes most people a few hours. Each ball goes from one hand to the other in what's supposed to be a graceful arc. It's frustrating at first, and you spend most of your time picking up balls. Eventually you get the hang of throwing one ball before you catch the previous one, and you develop a rhythm that becomes automatic. There are lots of variations which take ages to master, but the underlying idea is straightforward enough. I did a lot of practising, and soon I was able to keep a pattern going for as long as I wanted.

Naturally I wanted to move on, to develop my skills further. Four balls seemed the obvious next step, but juggling even numbers of balls is quite different from odd numbers. Instead of tossing each ball from one hand to the other, four-ball juggling consists of two independent patterns – one for each hand. When you throw two balls round in a circle with each hand at speed, it looks as if all four balls are crossing. In fact, they never do. I found this tricky, but after a few months I became able to do this too.

The crunch came with five balls. Because this is another odd-number pattern, each ball moves from hand to hand. It doesn't sound much more difficult than juggling three balls, but it is – by an order of magnitude. For a start, you have to be far more accurate in throwing and catching. You also have to throw all the balls high into the air in rapid succession, then start catching and throwing them again. I just couldn't do it. I practised for months and months, and to this day I've never cracked it. Even Adrian, who could juggle five balls in his sleep, didn't seem able to help. He tried approach after approach but I just couldn't get it. I was stuck at a threshold I couldn't cross, a barrier I couldn't push through.

Repetition is essential in any field, as we've seen. Doing time is necessary in order to progress, but on its own it's not enough – it's all too easy to tread water without moving forward. Once you've got the hang of an aspect of your work, whether taking blood, making pocket flaps or anything else, you have to push through an invisible barrier to reach the next level. This is what Ericsson means by sustained deliberate practice *with the intention to improve.*

Each time you come up against one of these invisible barriers and get through it, you move a little further along the path to becoming expert. Whenever that happens, you quickly focus on the new challenge and forget how hard you worked to get there. If it doesn't happen, you remain stuck, like me trying to juggle five balls.

If I'd wanted to become a professional like Adrian, I'd have found a way to push through that barrier. But for me, juggling was relaxation, not a career. Once I'd gained a reasonable proficiency, I never worked hard enough to move on to the next stage. I had reached Ericsson's 'stable performance asymptote' and stayed there.

My work in medicine was different, however. Even though I found taking blood difficult, I was determined to keep going and master it. I kept practising, and in the end I got there.

Getting there

Back to Manchester in 1974. I'm struggling to put in an intravenous cannula and set up a drip on my emergency patient and I'm scared stiff. But that day I'm lucky. An experienced nurse helps me assemble the giving set and run through some fluid. My patient has veins that even a novice could find, and I strike gold at my first attempt. Blood flashes back, I slide the cannula into the patient's vein and the nurse helps me connect the tubing. 'Thank you, Doctor,' the patient says gratefully. Being called 'Doctor' when I'm just a student makes me feel proud, though also like an imposter.

Even my limited experience doing the bloods had allowed me to perform a different procedure on my first go, at short notice and in an emergency. That's what repetition makes possible. But whatever your area of activity, there's no shortcut to doing time. You can't cheat the clock. Knowing this can be helpful, because if you're slow it doesn't mean you're stupid. It's just that the skills of 'doing' have different rules, and the kind of knowing that is required develops at a different speed from the knowledge of facts or figures. Remember, during those dark, dispiriting times when you seem to be standing still, that stuff is going on inside which will eventually come to fruition. You just have to keep going.

One afternoon over tea, I told an experienced doctor on my team how difficult I'd found my first round of doing the bloods. She looked at me blankly. She could no longer understand what it was like to flounder around with such an apparently simple task – simple, that is, to her. By then she had taken blood so often that it was second nature. She had made a transition and couldn't see the gulf I was facing. Some time later, the same thing started happening to me.

I got the hang of the bloods. I worked out a system for keeping track of my specimen bottles, lab forms, syringes and needles. I could put up drips and manage the kit. I was gaining confidence in approaching patients I'd never met, and I was coming to terms with causing a necessary discomfort. I'd begun to join a community of practice. I was even able to help a junior student myself, giving them tips about how to do what I'd once found so difficult. Already those difficulties were starting to blur and fade. I couldn't put myself back in their position because I'd moved forward. I'd taken a step along the journey to becoming expert.

I learned something else from doing the bloods, something even more important which I didn't notice at the time. While I was concentrating on getting round all those patients to take their blood before the lab closed, I wasn't only learning marksmanship with a syringe needle; I was learning to talk to people and to listen, to gain their trust and get them to let me into their personal space. I was learning to steel myself so I could carry on, even when I was causing pain and I knew that someone more experienced could have done it better. I was learning to relate to patients, to navigate the space between myself and another person – someone who was anxious, uncertain and vulnerable. In a nutshell, I was learning to become a doctor.

Becoming a doctor, a tailor or a hairstylist involves more than just learning skills. You have to start *thinking* like a doctor or a tailor or a hairstylist, and not just doing the things those people do. Something was changing inside me. When somebody called me 'Doctor', I didn't feel sheepish. I turned around and asked, 'How can I help?'

4. Using your senses

It's the middle of the night at Baragwanath Hospital in 1982. I'm 'first call' for our surgical unit and I'm starting a laparotomy. My patient is Poppy. She's twenty-six years old and has typhoid. It's a terrible disease and it has punched holes in Poppy's intestine. Her whole system is septic and she's very sick. By this time I've done a lot of laparotomies, but I've never seen typhoid before. As soon as I make my first incision, I can see I might be in trouble. Poppy's abdominal cavity is full of pus, there are perforations in the gut, and intestinal contents are pouring out. Everything looks a mess and it smells terrible.

The textbooks make operating on perforated bowel sound pretty straightforward. You remove the diseased segment – 'resect' it, in surgical terminology – then connect the ends to make a watertight join or anastomosis. To do this, you first decide how much you need to cut out, then you identify the arteries and veins which supply that segment. You clip, cut and tie the vessels and check there's no bleeding. Then you put clamps across the bowel, divide it with a scalpel, remove the diseased section, bring the remaining ends together and join them with needle and thread or a stapling device.

This, of course, makes it sound simpler than it really

is. For one thing, you have to ensure that you've cut away just enough to reach healthy bowel and that the edges have a good blood supply. If you get this wrong, the join won't heal. It may even leak in the coming days, which can be disastrous. But it can be difficult to tell at the time whether the blood supply is good or not.

The problem with Poppy is that everything's wrong. Her abdominal organs don't look like anything I've seen before. I can't tell where diseased bowel stops and healthy bowel begins. Most of the patients I've been operating on are young, fit men who have been stabbed. Though there's serious damage, their organs are generally healthy. Typhoid changes all of that. My usual reference points have vanished and I'm in a bind.

Poppy's abdomen not only looks and feels different from what I've seen before; it behaves differently too. Typhoid gives human bowel the consistency of wet blotting paper. Every time I touch Poppy's intestine, it starts to fall apart. Though the anatomical structures are familiar, their materiality is weird. Too little tension on any join, and the anastomosis will leak; too tight, and the sutures will tear out. Each could have catastrophic consequences, so I have to get it just right. But how can I recognize what 'just right' means? How much intestine should I remove? How hard can I pull it? What if handling it makes things worse? The usual cues no longer hold. I'm having to make judgements based on what I see, feel and smell; on things the textbooks can't tell you. I'm having to reconfigure what I thought I knew – and fast. The stakes are high and I'm terrified. How do I decide what to do?

By this time, I've got some way along my path towards becoming expert. I've been through the initial steps as an Apprentice – first as a doctor and now as a surgeon. I've struggled with knowing nothing and feeling out of my depth in everything I do. Now I'm building my internal library of sensations, and really getting to know my materials and tools. I've laid the groundwork through doing time. I've read books and watched other people. I've gained a sense of what normal organs look and feel like. I know a lot about what to do, but much less about how to do it. In this chapter, we'll explore what it means to acquire that knowledge of doing and what happens around its edges. Because now I'm at the limit of my experience. With Poppy, I'm in hostile territory.

'You just know'

This tension between knowing what you should do and being able to do it is something that many experts describe. It's the same in the calmer world of wood engraving. Andrew Davidson has been an engraver for forty years. Wood engraving is centuries old, a combination of craftsmanship and art. When I visited Andrew in his home at the end of a rutted lane in England's rural Gloucestershire, he was finishing the illustrations for a Harry Potter book. I watched him incising a boxwood block, using engraving tools with names that go back hundreds of years. He laid out spitstickers, scorpers, burins and burnishers, like a surgeon's instruments. I heard the crunch as each tool bit into the smooth, hard wood. Andrew calls this 'painting with light'. Even without looking he knows when the depth of each mark is right, because he can feel and hear it.

Then came the printing. Using a massive nineteenth-century cast-iron Albion press, Andrew arranged the engraved woodblock, face up. He squeezed black ink from a tube onto a flat stone block, then moved a miniature roller to and fro, coating its cylindrical surface with an even layer. Getting the right thickness of ink is crucial. Andrew judges this by ear, not by eye. 'As you roll it over the stone, it should sound like the air going out of a Lilo,' he explained, 'not like the sound of chips frying.'

Andrew inked the woodblock, placed a sheet of paper over it, then used the press's balanced handle to apply just the right amount of pressure for the right amount of time. He raised the handle, peeled off the paper and examined the result. Then he shook his head, inked the block again, put in a fresh sheet of paper and repeated the process until it was right.

Recognizing what's 'right' has taken Andrew decades to learn. It's not something he can put into words because it's about sensation. He's not just using his hands, but 'reading' the press with his whole body; responding to the feel, sound and smell of his materials. He knows exactly the amount of pressure to apply. But when he let me have a go, I felt clueless. I was just pulling a heavy lever, with no idea what I was aiming to achieve.

This multisensory awareness is what experts depend on. When you dissect the craft of any expert, you'll find something similar. Yet when you talk to these experts, they struggle to explain. They say things like, 'Well, you just do what's right – you just *know*.' But unless you've spent the years they've spent doing it, you can't 'just know'. And even then, you never really get there. Andrew explained it to me like this: 'For more than forty years I've been trying to make the perfect print from a woodblock. I never have, and I know I never will. But I'll never stop trying.'

Andrew puts his finger on another important principle. His materials perform best at their limits, when they are stretched almost to breaking point. His finest work will often be at the edge of what his materials will tolerate, at the point of greatest risk – just as Poppy's gut required my best surgical effort. But how can you tell where the limit is? I found out more about that from another expert, this time in the field of ceramics.

Thin materials on the verge of collapse

Duncan Hooson teaches pottery at several London art schools. He's a gifted tutor as well as an outstanding artist, and he's published a textbook on ceramics. Though some of his students are highly skilled, many are complete beginners. When I first met Duncan, we talked about how far you can push your materials before you go too far. Duncan calls this 'working with thin materials on the verge of collapse'. It's a crucial skill for every expert, and it's what I struggled with as I operated on Poppy.

When you watch an expert like Duncan, his work looks effortless. First he 'wedges' a lump of clay, thumping it like a baker working dough. Then he starts his potter's wheel and slaps the clay onto it. As the wheel picks up speed, he applies a little pressure here, a gentle finger there, and the clay morphs into the curved base of a vase. When he gets to the top of the vessel he draws out its neck by gently pinching the clay between his fingers. When the thickness is just right, he stops pinching. As simple as that.

But of course it isn't really simple at all. This pinching is a crucial operation. Not enough, and the neck stays lumpen and inelegant, too thick for the rest of the vase. Too much, and the clay collapses, unable to sustain its own weight. Then you have to start all over again. Duncan makes this look effortless, a wordless knowledge of just how far he can go. He has built up an awareness of what it feels like to be on the verge of collapse, a sensitivity that tells him when to stop and when to carry on a little further.

Duncan's work only looks effortless because of his decades of practice. Like the other experts in this book, he has been through years of doing time, making thousands of pots and vases. That was his equivalent of taking blood, making pocket flaps or creating flat stone surfaces. Most of his students haven't done that. They have to learn to notice when they're approaching a limit, to recognize that fine line between not far enough and too far. They have to learn to be attentive.

For Duncan, this is a bodily understanding. Potters do much of their work directly with their hands and fingers. Sometimes they use tools – for scraping, separating a pot from its base, inscribing patterns. But most of the time they are in an intimate, unmediated contact with their clay. They develop an exquisite sensitivity. It's this dialogue between Duncan's body and his materials that allows him to make continual adjustments. He may notice that his clay is too dry, too soft or too squidgy. This isn't something that can be defined. Unlike divisions on a ruler, there is no codified, objective 'scale of squidginess'. Interpreting squidginess requires an internal library, stocked through constant practice.

But it's not only physical materials that can become thin, teetering on the verge of collapse. Whether you're drafting a report, managing conflict in your workplace, practising a piece of music or writing computer code, completion and collapse are never far apart. Too little, and it's not enough. A fraction further, and it's over the edge.

In surgery, this physical knowing is crucial. You learn to 'read' the landscape you're working in, the organs you're touching. Like the sensation of the road when you're driving – mediated through the suspension of the car and felt through the seat of your pants – this is a combination of body and instruments. As a surgeon I developed similar skills to those Duncan uses when he is shaping the neck of a vase. You see with your fingers and your hands. You sense the squidginess directly. You gauge how springy and healthy an organ feels. You register when it's soggy and waterlogged, abnormally stiff, or overheated. You get a sinking feeling when an organ is starved of its blood supply and has the coldness of ischaemia. You feel the crackle of air in places it shouldn't be. You have a sense of how robust or vulnerable someone's tissue is. You develop an awareness of impending danger when you get too close to the limit.

I find this with words too. I spend a lot of time writing essays for journals and giving talks. There, too, is a fine line to tread. Too few words and it doesn't make sense. Too many and it becomes boring. At various points this book has behaved like a thin material on the verge of collapse. If I make a chapter too short or too long, or include too many examples, all of a sudden the whole thing falls apart. Success depends on recognizing the border, on having the skill to stop just before you cross it. Everyone I've spoken to finds parallels in their own lives – from thickening a sauce in the kitchen to taking the final millimetre off a wood carving. They are all developing their sense of where that verge of collapse lies.

Mechanic's feel

In the operating theatre with Poppy I'm up against thin materials on the verge of collapse in surgery, though I didn't think of it in those terms at the time. I know the steps of the procedure I need to do and I've done it lots of times before. I know what organs should look and feel like, and I can find my way around a normal patient's abdomen blindfolded. But Poppy's intestines are like nothing I've ever encountered.

I haven't bargained for distorted materiality. Anatomy in a cadaver is one thing and anatomy in a living person is another, but the anatomy of disease is different again. I haven't yet developed enough experience to know how far to go, to understand what Poppy's intestine will permit me to do. If I don't cut out enough, she'll die of her disease. If I cut out too much, her digestive system won't be able to function. I need to find the point of imminent collapse, and walk up to the border without crossing it. How do I decide where that border lies? I run her intestine between my fingers, scrutinizing its colour and gauging its texture as I weigh up where to cut.

Recognizing the materiality of what you are working with is central to becoming expert. Robert Pirsig talks about this in his classic 1974 book *Zen and the Art of Motorcycle Maintenance*. He calls it 'mechanic's feel'. He writes:

The mechanic's feel comes from a deep inner kinaesthetic feeling for the elasticity of materials. Some materials, like ceramics, have very little, so that when you thread a porcelain fitting you're very careful not to apply great pressures. Other materials, like steel, have tremendous elasticity, more than rubber, but in a range in which, unless you're working with large mechanical forces, the elasticity isn't apparent.

With nuts and bolts you're in the range of large mechanical forces and you should understand that within these ranges metals are elastic. When you take up a nut, there's a point called 'finger-tight' where there's contact but no take-up of elasticity. Then there's 'snug', in which the easy surface elasticity is taken up. Then there's a range called 'tight', in which all the elasticity is taken up. The force required to reach these three points is different for each size of nut and bolt, and different for lubricated bolts and for locknuts. The forces are different for steel and cast iron and brass and aluminium and plastics and ceramics.

But a person with mechanic's feel knows when something's tight and stops. A person without it goes right on past and strips the threads or breaks the assembly.

All the experts I've talked to know about mechanic's feel, and the challenges of thin materials on the verge of collapse. Whether it's Derek the taxidermist skinning a baby vole, Andrew the engraver capturing the shimmer of twilight on a lake, or Joshua the tailor moulding the fall of a lapel, we all depend on what the books call 'embodied knowing'.

In the operating theatre with Poppy and her typhoid

perforations, I had to use all my mechanic's feel. I readjusted my sense of how hard I could pull and how much tension I could place on her fragile intestines. Gingerly, I tried to isolate a segment of bowel using my usual technique. It came to pieces in my hand. I realized I'd have to be much more careful. I liked to think I was a gentle surgeon, but I had to recalibrate. I couldn't afford to make things worse.

One of the reasons it takes so long to become expert is that you have to become familiar with variation, not just an 'ideal' state. You have to deal with materials that are old, fragile, recalcitrant, unpleasant to touch, smelly or even dangerous. When I was operating on Poppy I was dealing with familiar materials in an unfamiliar state, like the rusted-up screws or corroded components of a motorcycle. I had to widen my sense of mechanic's feel to account for departures from the norm.

As you struggle with the basics – taking blood without getting your specimens jumbled up; inking a woodblock without causing a blot – you gradually become accustomed to the physicality of your work. With time, that work becomes less a matter of conscious attention and more a matter of routine. Your fingers stop being so clumsy, your materials don't seem so intransigent. You become increasingly aware of the intersection between you and what you're doing. This feeling doesn't reside wholly in you or your materials; it's a dialogue.

The language of the senses

We hardly ever use just one sense at a time. And while we think of touch, sight, hearing, smell and taste as if those 'Aristotelian five' were the only senses we have, neuroscientists and philosophers talk of a multitude of senses – perhaps as many as twenty-five. They distinguish between exteroception (recognizing information that comes from outside the body) and interoception (information from the body itself, about balance, orientation, or the hidden workings of our physiology). Becoming an expert requires integration between these outer and inner worlds. Sensory engagement is what turns looking into seeing, listening into hearing, touching into feeling, sniffing into smelling and tasting into savouring. Yet the information we get from our senses is not fixed. It can be shaped by our mental and physical state – by excitement, tiredness, hunger or stress.

Even thinking about the Aristotelian five, traditional distinctions between modalities are not clear-cut. We may not experience synaesthesia in a formal way, but our senses still cross over. As a surgeon I learned to see with my fingers. With my hands deep inside someone's abdominal cavity, I would build a picture of that patient's organs, learning to recognize what felt right and what felt wrong in territories of the body I could touch but couldn't see. This happens with all kinds of materials. Not only are silk and flannel different from one another, but each piece of silk has its idiosyncrasies and so does each piece of flannel. A novel isn't the same as a PhD thesis, though they are both book-length pieces of writing.

Each sense has its own characteristics too. Touch, for instance, has an immediacy that vision and hearing lack. Looking and hearing are sometimes described as 'distal' senses. If someone is out there and you see them, they don't necessarily see you. It's the same with hearing. But touch is 'proximal'. If you feel something, it 'feels' you, because you're in direct contact. It responds to your touch, even if it's inanimate. In medicine, this is especially obvious. You can't examine a conscious patient without them being aware of you touching them. It's the same whenever your work involves other people. You are conveying information at the same time as receiving it, whether you realize that or not. Even as an apprentice, Fabrice the hairstylist was conveying information about himself every time he washed a client's hair and touched their scalp.

Noticing your materials requires you to 'tune in' to your senses. This takes practice. It's easy to block out sensory information, to look without seeing, hear without listening and touch without feeling. Noticing means being present, being *attentive*. At the same time, you must be aware of the intersection between your materials and yourself. Experts do more than notice. They interpret and make sense. They respond to what they perceive. They act.

The philosopher Martin Heidegger captured this elegantly in one of his late lectures:

A cabinetmaker's apprentice, someone who is learning to build cabinets and the like, will serve as an example. His learning is not mere practice, to gain facility in the use of tools. Nor does he merely gather knowledge about the customary forms of the things he is to build. If he is to become a true cabinetmaker, he makes himself answer and respond above all to the different kinds of wood and to the shapes slumbering within wood – to wood as it enters into man's dwelling with all the hidden riches of its nature. In fact, this relatedness to wood is what maintains the whole craft.

The same applies to whatever area of work you are becoming expert in. Heidegger's 'relatedness to wood' applies equally to cloth, hair or boilers. You have to become connected to the materials you work with, attending to their subtleties and nuance.

It's the same with surgery. Living organs are not inert like those in the dissecting room; they have their own characteristics and personality. Nothing keeps still. The ureter 'vermiculates' if you prod it, moving like an earthworm. Healthy intestines writhe. Bowel is not just bowel, any more than cloth is just cloth, or stone is just stone. The small intestine of a healthy twenty-year-old involved in a car accident is very different from that of a fragile ninety-year-old with diabetes, let alone a patient like Poppy.

Over time, you get to know the ways of your materials.

You develop respect and affection for them, even when you find them frustrating. But, as we've seen, just doing things over and over again is not enough. Duncan Hooson's ability as a potter is not based on repetition alone. It's what the repetition has led to that counts. He's developed a sensitivity, an ability to 'read' what is happening between his fingers, his body at the potter's wheel and the clay he's shaping. He's gained an ability to recognize early signals of imminent collapse and take action while there's still time. He does this by attending to his physical world, by being present.

In whatever it is that you do, there are analogues to Duncan's fingers, his body at the wheel and the clay he's shaping. To improve, and later to become expert, you must develop the ability to maintain presence, even when your materials seem to be falling apart around you. Nobody can fully convey what something feels like when you touch it; you have to experience it for yourself. Textbook descriptions are largely useless – words alone can't capture when something is 'just right'. In surgery they say things like 'ensure that the anastomosis is under the minimum tension possible' or 'remove as much as necessary but no more than is required'. Unless you have a lot of experience, this gets you nowhere. It only makes sense if you already know what it means. And that knowledge comes through doing, through experiencing the sensations of materiality and by getting it wrong.

That's what tells you when you're dealing with thin materials on the verge of collapse.

Listening to your body

When I was operating for long hours at a stretch, working through the night with patients who had been stabbed and shot, I'd notice myself becoming clumsy. Instruments wouldn't do what I wanted, needles would slip out of my grasp, and I started dropping swabs. At first this just made me irritated with myself. Later, I learned to recognize that irritation as a marker of fatigue, a signal that I needed a break. I didn't actually feel tired, because of the adrenaline rush which emergency surgery creates, but my performance was starting to degrade.

Experts become adept at reading their own bodies as well as the materials they work with. They notice, interpret and act on small signals that their concentration is starting to lapse. They register when they themselves are becoming thin materials on the verge of collapse.

This doesn't only happen in the operating theatre. Like many people, I write on a computer. For years I've done this almost without thinking, the keys an extension of my fingers. But it wasn't always like that. When I was a teenager, my parents made me go on a two-week course in touch-typing. This was the era of mechanical typewriters, before word processors had arrived on the scene. At that time, typing was usually done by professionals, who had been on courses lasting a year or two. Programmes like that involved endless practice, bashing out boring exercises week after week and doing speed tests. My course was quite different. It consisted of ten one-hour sessions, one each weekday for a fortnight, and that was it. No preparation, no practising between sessions, no homework. That's why I agreed to do it.

Every day I sat in a class of twenty people, each of us in front of a typewriter with blanked-out keys so there was no temptation to look at our hands. The 'home keys' were red and that's where our fingers needed to hover, returning each time after reaching out to press a letter. All the other keys were grey. A similar keyboard was projected on a huge screen at the front. During the lessons a pre-recorded voice would intone letters in a slow monotonous rhythm, at two-second intervals. Each letter's key would light up on the screen, and we would have to press the corresponding key on our own machine. As the lessons went on the speed increased, moving from random letters to simple words. By the end of the course, I could type at a respectable speed, with a steady rhythm and without looking at the keyboard at all. It was one of the most useful things I ever learned.

Later, though, I realized that my accuracy and speed were not constant. They varied with how I was feeling. When I was tired, I would make unforced errors and have to go back and erase them with correcting fluid. That took a long time and interrupted my flow. I became irritated with myself and the typewriter, and things would go downhill. As I discovered later in the operating theatre, that irritation was telling me I needed to stop. Yet this capacity to 'read' my body took a long time to develop. Even now when I'm writing it takes me a while to recognize the signals. My concentration is a thin material on the verge of collapse; sometimes I need to take a break.

Pirsig says something similar in *Zen and the Art of Motorcycle Maintenance* when he describes hiking in a canyon in Montana with his son Chris as they're both getting very tired. 'By about three in the afternoon,' he writes, 'my legs start to get rubbery and it's time to stop. I'm not in very good shape. If you go on after that rubbery feeling you start to pull muscles and the next day is agony.' Pirsig has an awareness of his own body in that context and makes decisions accordingly.

Experts develop an internal instrument panel that allows them to monitor what is happening at that nexus between hands, tools and materials. They know when to push on and when to take a break. Anyone who has spent time learning a skill will be familiar with that experience. As I've spent time with experts in different fields, I've kept hearing the same story. They've all developed a relationship with the materials and tools they work with. Everything has 'materiality', the physical characteristics that determine its behaviour. Becoming expert involves recognizing the subtleties of this material world.

By spending time with materials, you come to understand their nature and learn about your own. As I've pointed out in my example of typing, even apparently abstract activities like writing have a strong physical element. If you focus your attention on your body, you become aware of the feel of the pen in your hand, the texture of the paper you're writing on, or irregularities in the computer keyboard under your fingertips and the click of the keys as you type. Yet in descriptions of expert practice, the senses of touch, hearing and smell are often overlooked.

Developing this awareness is a long process and there are no shortcuts. Through familiarity, however, you will begin to understand how far you can push things and when you need to back off. Gaining fluency in the language of your senses is the next step on the path to becoming expert.

The difference between looking and seeing

As a trainee surgeon, I remember assisting my consultant in an elective parathyroidectomy – an operation to remove the parathyroid glands. These are curious structures, usually (though not always) found in the neck. I'd learned about them when studying anatomy, but never seen them in real life. They are called parathyroids because they commonly sit alongside the thyroid gland, but functionally they have nothing to do with it. Instead they produce a hormone for regulating calcium metabolism. Sometimes they go wrong and have to be removed. Usually there are four of these small pinkish structures, but they are notorious for being variable in size, number and position, and for being difficult to recognize during surgery.

My chief made an incision into the patient's neck, then began exploring the complex anatomy underneath. The neck is full of delicate structures which have to be peeled apart, making sure that tiny nerve twigs are preserved. He was a taciturn surgeon and didn't explain what he was doing, but after a while he grunted, 'There they are, see?' and carried on dissecting. I had no idea what he was talking about. I couldn't see anything remotely resembling a parathyroid. But I didn't want to seem ignorant, so I kept quiet. After what seemed like a long time, I suddenly saw what he was working on: small clumps of tissue I had completely missed. Despite learning the anatomy from textbooks, teaching it to medical students in the dissecting room and having operated on a lot of necks myself, I hadn't seen what was right in front of me.

Looking – really looking – requires a lot of effort. It doesn't just happen when you open your eyes and point them at something. It's an active process that demands your full attention. For many of us, this kind of looking doesn't come naturally; it's a skill that has to be nurtured. Noticing what is really there, rather than what you expect to see, demands a relaxed eye, lots of time and infinite patience.

As a medical student I was taught how to carry out a physical examination; I memorized a sequence. First you look, then you touch, and only then do you listen with your stethoscope. 'Inspection, palpation, percussion, auscultation', the textbooks called it. Whatever the patient's symptoms, the mantra never varied. Your consultant would pillory you if you failed to do things in the right order, if you left out a step or brought out your stethoscope too soon. The cornerstone was using your eyes: really looking.

I learned to demonstrate that I was looking by ostentatiously standing away from the patient's bedside, hands behind my back, and describing what I saw according to a formula. 'The patient is a well-nourished man of seventy, lying quietly with no evident distress. Fingers show no evidence of clubbing, tremor or splinter haemorrhages. The accessory muscles of respiration are not in use . . .' Only after reciting a checklist of physical observations could I move on to palpation, to touching the patient, putting my hand on their chest, abdomen or limbs. Even then I was taught always to look at the patient's face while I was touching them, alert for tiny signals that I might be causing pain or discomfort.

I didn't understand the value of this discipline when it was being dinned into me. It seemed a waste of time. Surely if a patient had abdominal pain, you needed to put your hand on their abdomen to find out if they were tender, not spend ages looking at their face to see if their lips were blue. After all, that's how the doctors I was working with did it. They cut to the chase. They palpated the patient's abdomen and put their stethoscope onto the chest straight away. Or so it seemed.

In reality, these experienced clinicians *had* made observations first, but so rapidly that I hadn't spotted them doing it. Almost always they noticed more than I did. When they asked me to present a patient, they'd say things like 'And what about the asymmetry of this patient's fingernails?' or 'Why do you think his breathing is uneven?' – things I hadn't even registered. They would put these clues together to make a diagnostic story.

Eventually, I realized that this discipline of observation was essential. Seeing the patient as a person – rather than narrowing my focus down to one area of their body – stopped me jumping to conclusions. It was about learning to *see*. That was the difference between me and my consultant during the parathyroid operation. He had learned to look in a way that I hadn't. I had no reference points and I hadn't 'tuned in' my eyes. I had never seen the parathyroids in a living patient and I didn't yet know what to look for.

For experienced clinicians, attentive looking has become second nature. Yet this process can unravel under stress. Every year at my university I'm an examiner for the medical students' finals, the last stage before they qualify as doctors. I watch the students physically examining patients and demonstrating the sequence they've been taught. Inspection, palpation, percussion, auscultation. They look, they touch, they listen. Then they make sense of the information they've gathered and present their conclusions. That's the theory, anyway.

One year, after watching a student peer at the patient,

then feel her pulse while looking at his watch, I asked him what he was doing. 'Measuring the pulse rate,' he replied. 'And what is it?' I asked. First he looked nonplussed, then aghast. He picked up the patient's wrist and started counting again. In the stress of the moment he had gone through the motions, but that was all. He had demonstrated the procedure he'd been taught, but hadn't engaged his brain or processed the information he'd gathered. He had looked without seeing, touched without feeling, felt the pulse without considering what it meant for that patient.

There's much less emphasis now on looking and touching in medicine. In the decades since I was a medical student, imaging technology has revolutionized clinical practice. Ultrasound, CT, MRI and PET scans show internal anatomy with astonishing precision. In many ways that's a huge improvement, providing detail that would have been unimaginable even a few years ago. But while it's tempting to farm out the looking to specialist radiologists trained to interpret images, there's a danger of losing touch with your patients, of missing the wider picture for each unique person. I've noticed this problem in many other fields of expertise. Relying too much on technology can blunt your senses, preventing you from seeing what's under your nose or responding to the individual you're with.

There's real value in the drill of slowing down and being systematic. Perhaps because we use our vision all the time, it's easy to take it for granted, to think that by glancing we have really seen. The term 'inspection' gives an identity to attentive looking, and frames it as an act that has to be performed deliberately.

Yet at an early stage in your career, there are dangers within an atomized approach. You can believe that going through the motions is the same as having grasped the point. This is the seductive effect of learning components without understanding the whole picture. Once you can make a good pocket flap or cut a straight fringe, you might believe that you know more than you do about making jackets or styling hair. You become over-confident, and sooner or later you come a cropper.

Slowing down

The Dreyfus brothers (Stuart, a mathematician, and Hubert, a philosopher) are widely known for their model of adult skill acquisition, published in their 1986 book *Mind Over Machine: The Power of Human Intuition and Expertise in the Era of the Computer.* They describe five stages, which they call novice, advanced beginner, competence, proficiency and expertise. Of the final stage, they say, 'When things are proceeding normally, experts don't solve problems and don't make decisions; they do what normally works.'

A decade later, the researchers H. G. Schmidt, G. R. Norman and H. P. Boshuizen pointed out that 'there are two separable levels or stages – a rapid, non-analytic dimension, which is used in the majority of problems, and a slower, analytic approach, applied to a minority of problems that present difficulties . . . neither is to be preferred, since both may lead to a solution'. In 2011, the Nobel Prize–winning author Daniel Kahneman described a similar idea in *Thinking, Fast and Slow*. He outlined what he calls System 1 and System 2 thinking. 'System 1', he writes, 'operates automatically and quickly, with little or no effort and no sense of voluntary control. System 2 allocates attention to the effortful mental activities that demand it.'

As a junior doctor, presenting patients to my consultant, I noticed how experienced clinicians would switch between modes of reasoning. Sometimes they would go through information sequentially, checking to spot things we might have missed. But for much of the time, they did things in a different way. On the twice-weekly ward round, my chief in his three-piece suit would stop at each patient's bedside, surrounded by his retinue of registrars, housemen, students and nurses. One of us would present the patient's case, summarizing the history, clinical findings and laboratory tests. Sometimes the problem was a difficult one and we hadn't found the diagnosis. At first, I thought that would mean the consultant would order more tests. Often, however, he would just stand quietly and look at the patient. Then he would ask a few questions, carry out a brief examination, then say, 'I wonder if we should consider . . .' Usually he'd suggest a diagnosis we hadn't thought of, and more often than not he was right. By looking rather than doing, he was showing us a different way of thinking.

We all have inbuilt biases which can skew our judgement. There's an old adage in medicine that the fracture you're most likely to miss on an X-ray is an unexpected second one – especially if the first one is obvious. When somebody has been in a road accident and has an obvious break of an arm or leg, it's easy to overlook more subtle fractures of the spine or the fingers. What we see is shaped by what we look for, and once we have found something that provides a plausible explanation, we stop looking. Kahneman points out the power of confirmation bias – the tendency we have to make evidence support what we want to believe. We jump to a conclusion, then move on. But as we become expert, we have to counteract this tendency.

Of course, everyone struggles with learning to look properly, to see what's really there. When Joshua was struggling with pocket flaps, he couldn't see why his master Ron said his work was wrong. It looked fine to Joshua. But Ron could tell by looking that it wasn't good enough, that it wouldn't lie properly or match the body of the jacket. Like my chief the parathyroid surgeon, and my fisherman friend who could see the fish in the bend of the river, Ron noticed things that less experienced people couldn't see.

It's surprisingly easy for your glance to skate over what's in front of you, like mine with the invisible fish. You can believe that you've looked properly, only to find later that you haven't. How many times have we checked over an email, only to find the spelling mistake after it's been sent? We tend to see what we think is there, rather than what actually is.

Drawing is a discipline that forces you to register what you see. Tiny details matter when you're drawing something, and a cursory glance is not enough. You have to let your gaze sink into what you're looking at, and fix it in your memory. The artist and embroiderer Fleur Oakes, one of my colleagues at the Art Workers' Guild, describes drawing as 'looking at something for longer than you normally would'. It's the looking that's the crucial part. Drawing helps you register what you see by connecting your eyes, your body and your brain.

Drawing has always been central to artists, whatever their specialism. In former times, the students at the Royal Academy of Arts, where I'm now the Professor of Anatomy, had a rigorous training which started by drawing plaster casts of classical statues. Only once they became proficient at that were they allowed to move on to life classes with living human models. At some art schools, tutors even positioned these life models upstairs and made their students put their easel in the basement. The students had to decide which aspects of the model to keep in their mind as they made each trip downstairs to add another detail. Although there's less focus on life drawing at art schools nowadays, many current experts went through that kind of rigour when they were training. But drawing isn't something that only artists do. It's just as useful in any other area of work.

Making a mark on paper forces you to home in on what is essential and think about the information you want to convey. We all use some form of drawing, whether we recognize it or not. If you're a pianist annotating a score, a lawyer sketching out an argument, a writer drafting a plot or a surgeon summarizing an operation in a patient's case notes, you'll almost certainly make marks on paper (or perhaps a screen) to communicate. Those marks become a way of distilling what is central and leaving the rest out.

Putting it all together

Back in the operating theatre with Poppy and her typhoid perforations, I'm bringing all my senses together. I'm tuning in to what her body is telling me. I'm reconfiguring the information I'm gathering through sight, touch and smell, and turning it into action. Although I'm out of my depth, I just have to do the best I can. Gingerly I go through the steps I've learned for a bowel resection. At every stage I'm treading on eggshells. I know I have to remove the areas that have perforated and cut back to healthy bowel. But what *is* healthy bowel? None of it looks healthy to me. Yet I need to preserve as much as possible.

In the end I have to make a decision and hope for the

best. I remove the segments of intestine that are beyond repair, then reconnect what's left as gently as I can. Eventually I close Poppy's abdomen, cross my fingers and ask the anaesthetist to wake her up. All through that night I keep checking on her to make sure she's stable.

As I'd suspected, that operation is just the first stage, and Poppy has a stormy post-operative course. The next day she becomes sicker. I take her back to theatre and remove some more intestine. The same thing happens again a few days after that. But eventually, after several weeks, she starts to recover. Soon we're able to move her from intensive care, disconnect her tubes and monitors, and wheel her to a bed on the general ward. Gradually, she starts to improve.

As she regains strength, I get to know Poppy better. I discover that she teaches English at a primary school in Soweto. Sometimes I sit next to her after the ward round for a few minutes. We talk about her plans and her ambitions, her family and the people she works with. In the weeks that follow, Poppy gradually builds up stamina. She starts to move around, first with the help of a nurse and then on her own. One day she takes a few steps into the sunshine. When I go past the ward after that, I often see her in a chair, reading. Eventually, at long last, she's fit enough to go home. Seeing her leave the hospital on her way back to her family and her classroom is something I'll never forget.

5. Space and other people

Back to Manchester Royal Infirmary, this time in 1976. It's the middle of the night and I'm fast asleep when my pager goes off. I'm a bit more experienced than when I started the bloods that Sunday morning in Chapter 3, though I'm still a medical student. Now I'm on my maternity attachment. I've been hauled out of bed to repair an episiotomy, the scissor cut into a woman's vagina which a midwife or obstetrician sometimes has to make during delivery. Its purpose is to release tension and minimize the chances of the baby's head splitting important structures such as the mother's anal sphincter. I'd learned to make these cuts when I was delivering babies. Then I found out the hard way that episiotomies are easier to make than to repair.

At that time, students were often called at night to sew up episiotomies, because nobody else wanted to do it. The excitement of bringing a baby into the world has simmered down, and the patient is usually exhausted. Of course, repairing a cut of this kind is crucial for the patient later on. It can have a major impact on a mother's continence and sexual function. I'm painfully aware that I need to get things right, but I'm not sure how.

From the few episiotomy repairs I've seen and done,

I know that when I arrive my patient will be in the lithotomy position, her feet in stirrups and her legs splayed. It's undignified and uncomfortable. Gowned and gloved, I'll sit between her legs with a portable operating light shining into her vagina. A nurse will put a sterile suturing pack with instruments, swabs, and small dishes for antiseptic solution onto a trolley next to me. After opening the pack and adding syringes, suture needles and local anaesthetic, the nurse will probably go away and do something else. I'll be left bleary-eyed and uncertain, staring into a dark cavity with blood oozing out, trying to make sense of my patient's anatomy, which won't look anything like the neat diagrams in my textbook. Then I'll have to remember what to do next.

Tonight my patient is Brenda. She's just given birth to Emma, her first baby. It's been a long labour and Brenda's exhausted. All she wants to do is sleep. But first there's her episiotomy to deal with. Shyly I introduce myself, trying to project a confidence I don't feel. 'Are you the doctor who delivered my baby?' she asks. Embarrassed, I stammer that I'm not yet a doctor, but I've been sent to sew up the cut her midwife had to make.

I take my seat between Brenda's legs, which are covered with green sterile drapes. Now I'm unable to see her face or make eye contact. I try to keep up a conversation, though it's difficult to do that and keep track of the procedure at the same time. I lapse into silence and focus on the task. I clean the perineal wound with antiseptic, then draw up some local anaesthetic and inject it slowly, as I've been shown. Brenda flinches and I realize that I was concentrating so hard on the procedure that I forgot to warn her that I'd be giving her an injection. My fragile confidence shatters and I feel mortified. I'm out of my depth, I can't see the expression of the person I'm talking to and my conversational landmarks have disappeared. Fortunately, this time, the nurse is still standing there. She holds Brenda's hand, tells her what I'm doing – then leaves me to get on with it. I need to suture the episiotomy and keep Brenda's confidence at the same time. How?

Developing mise en place

Part of this is about having a system to work with. When I started repairing episiotomies, I would shake the instruments out of their sterile pack and make a start. But each time I needed to pick up the needle-holder or grab another swab, I had to take my eye off my patient as I cast about amongst the clutter. When I looked again, the bleeding point would have vanished from view and I'd be back at square one.

One night, a kindly midwife saw me struggling. She came over and explained how to set things out in a logical sequence, so I could put my hand on what I needed, almost without looking. She asked if I was right- or left-handed, then showed me how to ensure the essential instruments were within easy reach. It made a huge difference, and from then on I laid out each pack in the same order. Eventually this became second nature, and I didn't even register I was doing it. In retrospect, this approach seems so obvious that I can't understand why I didn't realize it from the start. But at the time it wasn't obvious. None of the doctors ever mentioned it – it took someone else to point it out before the penny dropped. Even then, nobody gave it a name.

Years later, I learned that chefs describe this as 'mise en place', a French expression meaning 'organizing your workplace'. This is a fundamental principle in the high-pressure world of the restaurant kitchen, where everything depends on split-second timing and flawless coordination.

Mise en place is not just for the kitchen, though. It's how we can get into an unfamiliar car, identify the controls for headlights, indicators and horn, and drive. Yet small departures from what you are used to can still throw you off balance. An unfamiliar mise en place takes time to adjust to. Anyone who's driven a hired car will know how easy it is to find you've turned on the windscreen wipers instead of indicating a turn.

By now you're partway along the Apprentice section of the path towards becoming expert. You're becoming familiar with tools and materials, and you're learning how to read your own body as you work. But becoming expert is not just about tools and materials. It's about the way you interact with the world around you. To flourish within a system, you need to learn how it works and you need to fit in. That's what you do when you're starting.

As a beginner, it's easy to focus on individual tasks without noticing how your workplace is structured. By fitting into a way of working that is already there, you can overlook the importance of your environment. In any system, the materials and tools you work with have already been organized.

Experts don't work on only one task, so their focus is not just on the work in front of them. They have prepared things in advance and know where they've put them. They pay attention to how their workplace is arranged, to where their tools are, to what they will be doing next and how to lay their hands on what they need. Often they share their space with other people, and they have to notice and respect what others are doing. They put things back after using them, and they never use somebody else's tools. It's easy not to register their systematic approach, because it appears to be so effortless.

It was Jozef Youssef who explained to me about mise en place. Jozef is the founder and chef patron of Kitchen Theory, an experimental restaurant in north London which he describes as a design studio with a chef's table. Jozef's passion is what he calls 'multisensory gastronomy'. If you go there for a meal, you'll experience a succession of unusual courses, each engaging your senses in a different way. Jozef's creations play with vision, touch and hearing, as well as taste and smell. They invite you to see, hear, feel, smell and savour. Jozef only puts on his chef's table once a month, and then only for fourteen diners. The rest of the time he works with schools, industrial partners and academics to widen people's ideas about the world of food. Yet he started with a traditional training.

Like all the experts in this book, Jozef has been through the stages of doing time, using his senses and navigating space – in his case, in the kitchen and front of house. He's worked his way up through the hierarchy of fine dining, spending time in some of the world's leading restaurants. He's earned his stripes in Michelin-starred establishments. But wherever he's worked, mise en place is crucial. Everyone in a professional kitchen has to know exactly where everything is, from their knives and chopping boards to the ingredients for those last-minute touches as a dish leaves the kitchen for a table. Everyone depends on a shared understanding of how this works. Disrupting another cook's mise en place, like using another cook's knife, is a cardinal sin.

The need to be systematic is dinned into culinary students from day one. Mise en place starts with writing down the day's tasks in the order you'll perform them, specifying everything you'll need and making sure you can lay your hands on it at a moment's notice. When you join the 'brigade' of a professional kitchen, mise en place must have become second nature.

Jozef told me about the thousands of vol-au-vents he prepared at The Dorchester, a leading London centre of haute cuisine. The kitchen team were setting up for a high-profile function several weeks ahead. As Jozef finished making each batch of puff pastry, it was transferred to a freezer to wait for further preparation ahead of the big day, when he'd complete the vol-au-vents. These were just one element of one dish on a menu of five courses. Putting on a massive culinary event like that demands military precision. Remembering exactly where in the cold storage units he'd stored those earlier preparations was part of Jozef's mise en place. He couldn't afford to get it wrong.

Not many people work in Michelin-starred restaurants, but we all need mise en place. Whether we're keeping track of our tools in the garden shed or knowing where the spare light bulbs are in our house, mise en place is how we take the strain off our memory and minimize cognitive load. Anyone who has tried to memorize a string of phone numbers understands the value of an address book. It's the same with physical space.

Experts all develop systems which work for them. Derek Frampton's taxidermy workshop and Andrew Davidson's engraving studio didn't look highly organized to me. I wouldn't have known where they kept things. Yet both of them could lay their hands on whatever tool or material they needed, without even looking. There was a place for everything and everything was in its place; I just didn't know what those places were. Where they recognized order, I saw only clutter.

As a newcomer to their world, I could have easily

mistaken their set-up for the absence of any system at all. Someone looking at my writing desk would probably say the same. In both cases, that would be a mistake. These systems represent a distillation of years of experience, of experts having found what works for them.

Part of becoming expert is taking control of your environment. When I see Joshua in his workshop, he has his scissors, thread, tailor's chalk and cloth within easy reach. He and the other experts I've worked with all have their mise en place, though most of them don't use that term. Yet though a systematic approach is expected in almost every area of expert practice, this is seldom explained to novices. As I discovered when I was learning to repair episiotomies, as a beginner you are expected to know all this without being told. If you're lucky, someone helps you. But often no one does.

People often allow the arrangement of their workplace to be dictated to them; they forget they have agency to change it. Kirsty Flower, one of my colleagues at Imperial, told me it was only after years in the laboratory as a postdoctoral molecular biologist that she realized that she was a left-handed scientist working in a right-handed system. Since starting as an undergraduate, she had fitted into a system that was already there. Every time she picked up a pipette, she had to reach awkwardly across her workspace to the specimen bottles on the other side. Because she had always worked like that, it hadn't occurred to her to change her apparatus round. She was focusing on the work, not her system for doing it. Once she rearranged things, her work became much easier.

This highlights a characteristic of the Apprentice phase. You know that everyone else knows more than you, and you want to be part of the group. You don't want to look like an idiot, so you copy other people. But you are only mimicking what you've seen them do. You don't yet understand why or how they do it. So you often miss the finer points that later you'll come to rely on. You seldom have the confidence to shape your workplace, to impose your will on your environment – or even to adjust your chair to suit your height. Like me with my early attempts at episiotomy repair, you work with what you find rather than shaping it to your requirements.

It's easy to work in a mess at home, in your workshop, your kitchen or at your desk, as long as it's your mess. You know your own clutter, you have a sense of where you keep things, and it works for you. If you're working alone, it doesn't matter what your space looks like, as long as you can find what you need the moment you need it. But if you work with other people, there are reasons for maintaining an orderly space. Anyone who works in an open-plan office has had the experience of reaching for the stapler, only to find that someone has borrowed it and not put it back, or that someone has moved the pile of papers you were working on. This explains why sharing a workspace can be so stressful.

Often you only notice mise en place when it's disrupted. When someone comes to stay in your house and helps dry the dishes after supper, you often can't find utensils for weeks afterwards. Your visitors have put things in places that make sense to them but not to you. Objects have been misfiled, as if they were books on the wrong shelf in a library. It's bad enough if you can't find a saucepan. It's worse when you're working in a garage and you can't find the wrench you need because someone else hasn't put it back. In the operating theatre, of course, the stakes are especially high. There, the system for tracking tools is formalized, codified and directed by someone who is expert in exactly that – the scrub nurse.

The scrub nurse is a crucial part of the surgical team, responsible for all the instruments and materials used during an operation. They have to ensure that nothing is left inside a patient after a procedure is completed. Everything has to be counted in and counted out. Working closely with the surgeons, scrub nurses have to be able to lay their hands instantly on whatever instrument is needed and put it back there after use. They have to work within a consistent system that allows a scrub nurse from one theatre to move seamlessly to another. Yet they also customize their mise en place in a way that fits with how they personally like to work.

But the role of the scrub nurse goes far beyond handing over instruments and keeping track of them. Expert scrub nurses are constantly vigilant, paying close attention to the procedure and anticipating what will be needed. Like the highly experienced Sister Ramaphosa at Bara in Soweto, scrub nurses have years of experience. They can teach others in their team a huge amount. They are a crucial part of the community of practice of the operating theatre, using an unspoken language to communicate which even they are often unaware of.

When I did some research using video to analyse long-established surgical teams, I noticed a scrub nurse passing a pair of surgical scissors to the surgeon before he asked for them. Slowing down the film, you could see the surgeon holding out his hand, the nurse placing the scissor handles in his palm, the surgeon closing his fingers and starting to use the instrument, and only then saying, 'Scissors, please, Sister.' Playing the video for them afterwards, neither the surgeon nor the nurse had any recollection of what had happened. They had worked together for so many years that their actions had become instinctive. Old-school surgeons I worked for would even say, 'For heaven's sake, Sister, give me what I *want*, not what I asked for,' relying on that unspoken rapport that only comes from a long collaboration. This is the inheritance of a strong, well-organized mise en place.

Making a harpsichord

Joining an organization or working in a group allows you to benefit from having a mise en place that has developed over several years – or even, as in the case of surgery, over centuries. But if you've ever tried to teach yourself something without the help of others, you're likely to have suffered from having to build your own mise en place without the requisite context.

I learned the piano as a child, though not very well. I've always loved baroque music, and for years I had a yen to play the harpsichord. When I was a GP, I thought I'd take the plunge and get one. But harpsichords are expensive and I couldn't justify buying one before I knew if I'd like playing it. My compromise was to build one myself from a kit. Even a kit was almost more than I could afford, and would involve uncertainty and risk. I had no idea if I could even finish it.

After a lot of research, I decided on one made by John Storrs. He had trained as an engineer before going into musical instrument design, and he used that background to ensure that the mission-critical parts of the harpsichord assembly were foolproof – the spacing of the strings, the holes in the wrest plank for the tuning pins, those parts where a hair's breadth of error would result in an unplayable instrument. The parts that required endless patience but limited ability – assembling the jacks and fitting their horsehair bristles; sanding down ebony and bone keys; scraping plectra – he left to each customer.

The kit was based on a seventeenth-century instrument by Hans Ruckers, a famous Flemish maker. It arrived at my house in boxes. We had a small house, so I evicted our younger daughter from her tiny bedroom and turned it into a temporary workshop. There were two slim instruction booklets, one of words and the other of diagrams.

My main problem with building that instrument was that I had no idea what I was aiming for. I had to interpret instructions written by someone who already knew what I didn't. I had no one to help me recognize thin materials on the verge of collapse, no one to advise me about mise en place.

Although a harpsichord is quite small – much shorter than a grand piano, a fraction of its weight and with fewer notes – a lot goes on under the bonnet. The instrument I was making had three strings for each key. Each of those strings has its own jack: a thin slip of wood that sits on the far end of the key and plucks the string with a plectrum when you press down on the key. Each plectrum is seated in a tiny pivoted tongue in the jack, allowing it to pluck the string on the way up but slide silently past it on the way back. The damper, a small square of red felt, fits into a groove in the side of each jack and stops the string sounding once you release the key. It all has to be minutely adjusted.

There were almost two hundred of these jacks. Each of the steps – fitting the tongue, filing a tiny groove for the hog's hair bristle, cutting the damper felts, inserting the plectra – had to be done almost two hundred times, and each involved a new learning curve. Again and again I went from cack-handed ignorance to weary familiarity – that cycle of doing time.

The only way I could keep track of these minuscule parts was by developing my own mise en place. In my daughter's tiny bedroom, I was working in a cramped space. My tray of tools wasn't much bigger than the trolley of instruments I'd used when I was a medical student suturing Brenda's episiotomy after she'd given birth to her baby Emma. I needed a similar sense of order.

A big problem was that I was working alone. I wasn't in a workshop surrounded by other apprentices. All I had were the components of the harpsichord I was going to assemble. I didn't have access to an inherited mise en place, the collective knowledge of generations of harpsichord builders or the shared wisdom of a group. There was no community of practice for me to fit into. I didn't even have an example of a harpsichord to refer to. All I could do was follow the sets of written and illustrated instructions. Most challenging of all, I didn't have a sense of what to expect. I tackled the project one stage at a time, not knowing how all the elements would fit together. Those instruction booklets were a map, but I had no guide.

Gradually, I started to get the hang of things. By the time I'd cut my umpteenth red felt damper, put the finishing touches to yet another ebony key slip, or wound another string from a coil of brass wire, I was becoming comfortable in my workshop and developing my 'mechanic's feel'.

Anyone who has embarked on a project will have experienced something similar. You have to think through the components you're going to need so you can put your hand on them quickly. Sometimes the challenges are physical, like repairing an engine, suturing an episiotomy or building a harpsichord. Sometimes they are more conceptual, like writing an essay or a book, where you need access to information you've researched and references you'll cite. Whatever your field, you need to organize your workspace. But workspace is only part of the picture.

Personal space and other people

As I assembled that harpsichord at home, I could arrange my workshop as I wanted it. I could design my own mise en place. I didn't get that design right first time, but the only person who suffered from my mistakes was me. But in my medical work, I was sharing space with my patients. Often I needed to examine them, to look at them closely and touch their bodies. This isn't a straightforward process, as I have discovered several times when the roles have been reversed and I've become a patient.

When I started working in London, I bought a motor scooter. One summer evening I was riding home with my visor up when something hit me in the face. I didn't know what it was, but I felt liquid trickling down my cheek and my vision in one eye was blurred. I thought the liquid might be toxic or corrosive, and I was terrified. I went straight to my local eye hospital. First I was seen by a junior ophthalmologist. He seemed as anxious as I was. Though he did all the right things clinically, this doctor's examination made me feel very uncomfortable. He put his face close to mine without any warning, shone a bright light in my eye, then turned my upper eyelid inside out and examined my eye with a slit lamp. I flinched and moved about, and the experience was unpleasant for us both.

Half an hour later I saw the consultant. The experience was completely different. She glided effortlessly into my personal space, unhurried and gentle. Although she did the same things as the trainee – shining a bright light, everting my eyelid, using a slit lamp – she did them in a different way. I felt confident, at ease, happy to let down my barriers and allow her in. Fortunately, it turned out that the liquid was water, and although there was some damage to my eye it recovered in the following weeks. But I've never forgotten her approach. To me, she demonstrated mastery.

Many of the experts in this book work at close quarters with other people. There's a special skill to entering someone else's personal space, that buffer zone which is bounded by an invisible 'second skin'. This notional space is different for each of us, and our brains continually reconfigure it depending on the social context. The rules and expectations for being comfortable when a stranger approaches you are complex. Shaking hands with someone you've never met is acceptable; holding hands is not.

Some experts – like doctors, dentists, opticians, physiotherapists, osteopaths and massage therapists – work with people's bodies all the time. Bodies are these experts' primary material, their equivalent of the potter's clay, the cabinetmaker's wood or the sculptor's stone. Other experts – like barbers, hairstylists, beauticians, tattoo artists and body piercers – do something similar, though in a non-clinical setting. Tailors, corsetmakers and hat designers work with people's bodies at one remove, creating clothes that can be put on and taken off. Others, such as restaurant waiters, close-up magicians and theatre performers, work in people's personal space without touching them at all. Experts in all these fields develop a confidence that you hardly notice.

That sense of ease is characteristic of experts who work with precious materials, whether people or things. It often astonishes me to see a violin virtuoso tuning up before a performance. Even when the instrument is a priceless masterpiece – a Stradivarius or a Guarneri – she will handle it with supreme confidence. She places it gently between her chin and shoulder, taking both hands away before turning the tuning pegs at the end of the violin. Anyone else would be terrified of dropping the instrument in the tension of the moment, but these experts are secure in their mastery. Working with people requires a similar confidence – respectful yet assured.

The neuroscientist Michael Graziano has been working on personal space for decades. He begins his 2018 book, *The Spaces Between Us*, like this:

We all have an invisible, protective bubble around us. Personal space, margin of safety, bad breath zone, duck-and-flinch buffer – whatever you call it, we have it constantly switched on like a force field. It comes in layers, some layers close to the skin like a bodysuit, others farther away like a quarantine tent. Elaborate networks in the brain monitor those protective bubbles and keep them clear of danger by subtly, or sometimes drastically, adjusting our actions. You walk through a cluttered room weaving effortlessly around the furniture. A pigeon swoops past your head in the street and you duck. You stand a little farther from your boss than from your friend, and much closer to your lover. Usually hidden under the surface of consciousness, occasionally rising into awareness, personal space affects every part of human experience.

Graziano points out that initial notions of personal space as a 'second skin' developed in the 1960s as a psychological and social phenomenon. Edward T. Hall's *The Hidden Dimension*, published in 1966, put forward the notion of 'proxemics', the author's way of interpreting 'man's use of space as a specialized elaboration of culture'. Hall was building on the work of Heini Hediger, a pioneering animal biologist who developed the field of 'zoo biology' – the science of wild animals kept in human care.

Hediger, who was the director of the Zurich Zoo, showed that animals in their natural environment live within relatively small bubbles of territory which they take with them when they move. He described different interaction distances between animals. For example, flight distance is the distance an animal will tolerate when confronted by a member of a different species before fleeing. Critical distance is the narrow zone separating flight distance from attack distance (when an animal being pursued will turn and go on the offensive). Personal distance and social distance relate to interactions between animals of the same species. These determine the normal spacing that animals maintain between themselves and others in their group.

Hall's insight was to apply these observations to humans. Although flight distance and critical distance have been largely eliminated, personal and social distance remain. He put forward four categories of distance – intimate, personal, social and public. These distances are not fixed but change with context. They delineate an exclusion zone, a region in which you don't want other people. Hall put it like this: 'it is in the nature of animals, including man, to exhibit behaviour which we call territoriality. In so doing, they use the sense to distinguish between one space or distance and another. The specific distance chosen depends on the transaction; the relationship of the interacting individuals, how they feel, and what they are doing.'

Since the 1980s there has been an explosion of interest in personal space in the world of experimental neuroscience. It turns out that the space surrounding the body has a special representation in the brain. Graziano's own experimental work, first with monkeys and more recently with humans, demonstrates a highly complex set of specialized 'multisensory' neurons which allow us to keep track of the location of things, even in the dark. He has shown how sets of behaviours – documented first with animals and their territories, then by social observation of humans – turn out to have a neuroscientific basis that is only now beginning to be unravelled. Graziano writes of a 'simulated bubble wrap', an invisible second skin surrounding the body that emphasizes nearby space while also registering what happens further away. But unlike Hall's original concept, there is no single giant envelope of space around the body. Every body part seems to have its own bubble. This system allows us to keep track of objects through sight, sound, touch and even memory. It depends on a well-defined set of brain areas and specialized neurons that have elegant properties. The result is to weld our senses together into a visual-auditory-tactile radar for nearby objects.

But our mechanisms for personal space don't only apply to people – we extend our peripersonal buffer zone around our tools as well. That's how we can use a fork or a screwdriver to 'sense' what it is doing and interpret the space around it. Using the example of a vacuum cleaner, Graziano explains how a person monitors the spaces around the entire wand 'to make sure it doesn't crash into furniture or doorways and knock over vases, injure the cat, or bruise your own legs'. To use a tool competently, he points out, you must process the space around it. It seems that our brains incorporate the tool into a body schema, creating a modifiable margin of safety that can be extended around a foreign object.

This helps to understand the importance of mise en place – the need for an ordered and familiar environment where much can be taken for granted. In such a set-up, we have reconfigured our peripersonal buffer zones so we can use our energy for the work in hand rather than trying to make sense of the space around us.

Personal space and performance

The need to navigate other people's personal space with sensitivity and skill is especially pressing in medicine. Clinicians work with patients, and this involves proximity, contact and physical examination. Experienced doctors negotiate this without even thinking about it. They have become comfortable not only with being close to people physically but with handling any part of a person's body. It's easy to lose sight of how difficult this skill is to acquire, though my experience with the trainee ophthalmologist brought it back. As a medical student, it took me a long time to learn how to move in and out of personal space without showing anxiety or embarrassment or transmitting that to my patients. I had to listen to their chests, palpate their abdomens, move their joints, peer into their eyes and ears. At first I felt acutely uncomfortable. But eventually this clinical touch became a natural part of every medical encounter.

Navigating personal space involves understanding how to respond. As a patient who has already experienced a clinical consultation, you know what to expect. There are conventions you've learned to recognize. It's like going to a classical music concert. There, you find your seat, sit quietly and wait for the performers to come on stage and begin. You don't break open a bottle of whisky, pass round bags of fried chicken, and start telling raucous jokes to the people in the row behind. And the rules are different at a football match or Glastonbury music festival.

These are unspoken patterns of behaviour which we have absorbed since childhood. When you go to the doctor, you know you may need to be examined, so you're not surprised when it happens. Yet entering a patient's personal space as a clinician is the equivalent of going into their house. Indeed, in any sphere of work where you deal with other people, you can't just barge in. You have to be invited. You have to show respect. If everyone takes their shoes off at the door, so should you.

Entering and leaving personal space with grace and respect requires practice. At first you may think that your own imperatives – to acquire information, say, or impress your teachers – take priority over the needs of your patient, colleague or customer. You may not think about their experience much at all, but instead focus upon yourself. Gradually, though, you start to shift from you to them, resetting your focus from yourself to the space between the two of you.

Working in personal space requires sensitivity and an ability to 'read' people. Skilled professionals are able to enter and 'inhabit' someone's personal space without causing discomfort or even much awareness. By being at ease in someone's personal space, you help to make them comfortable too. Experts make this look effortless, though everyone knows what an inept or ill-intentioned attempt feels like. It might be a waiter who looms over you, demanding your attention when you're not yet ready to order; or a colleague who stands behind you, reading what's on your computer screen while you type.

Fabrice the hairstylist learned this when he was an apprentice shampooing clients' hair. People are most aware of the personal space in front of them, because that's where they're looking. In the salon, things function differently. In order to work with their hair, Fabrice approaches his clients from the side or behind. They can see him in the mirror, of course, but he isn't directly confronting them. Approaching from the side, where the warning systems of personal space are less sensitive, makes connecting with someone much easier. Good waiters know this too. They don't approach diners directly but from the side, gauging and adjusting their distance as they read the tiny unconscious signals that show where the invisible boundary lies. That's what allows them to move in and out of personal space, reading the dynamics of each individual and group.

Many experts use an unthreatening preliminary manoeuvre to make contact and set the scene. For a hairstylist, that might be running their fingers through their client's hair. Joshua the tailor starts by walking round a customer, then explains that he needs to move closer to gauge the fit of the trousers or jacket. Sam Gallivan, a hand surgeon I work with, takes each patient's hand when they first meet in her clinic. During the usual shake, she holds on for a bit longer as they begin their conversation. After a few moments, she has assessed the range of movement in all the important joints of the patient's fingers and wrist without her patient even realizing it. And she has established a physical contact that sets the tone for the rest of the consultation.

Social and technical skills do not always go hand in hand, and their boundaries are not clear. Fabrice talks about colleagues who are brilliant at cutting and styling hair, yet lack the ease which keeps their clients coming back. Others are highly skilled at social interaction, but their technical and aesthetic powers are ordinary at best. Meanwhile Joshua speaks of cutting tailors whose social skills are outstanding, but whose suits are mediocre. And we've all encountered financial advisers who sound plausible but don't know much, or computer geeks who can fix any problem but won't look you in the eye. To become expert, you need both.

Getting in touch with my patients

Within personal space, much is conveyed through touch. Confidence, assurance and concern, or roughness, indifference and ineptitude; we recognize these in an instant. Yet fluency in the language of touch can't be taken for granted. It has to be attended to, worked at, practised and perfected. In all fields, this is a challenge. As we've seen, touch is proximal and acts in two directions. It's a language you need to learn, but it doesn't have a dictionary.

When I was at medical school, none of my teachers said, 'Roger, you need to learn how to enter and work within your patients' personal space, and to become fluent in the language of touch.' Nobody said that to Fabrice or Joshua either, and nobody explained it to Jozef when he started working in a team of chefs. We all absorbed these skills without realizing, as a by-product of other work. Those years of doing the bloods, chopping onions, sweeping the floor or measuring inseams helped us to develop the confidence to pass through someone's invisible second skin; to feel comfortable within their personal space and to make them comfortable in return. That took a long time for all of us. But we were aided in our efforts by having a system, a mise en place.

I'm back with Brenda and her newborn baby. It's the middle of the night, and I've almost finished suturing the episiotomy. I've found it stressful, though I've tried not to let that show. I know how important this repair will be for her and I want to do the best I can. I'm also becoming more confident in the two elements we've looked at – taking responsibility for my mise en place and working in someone's personal space. I've been aided on this occasion by experienced colleagues, essential members of the system I'm in. There was the midwife who showed me how to set out my trolley, and the nurse who talked to Brenda while I concentrated on my task.

I tie and cut the final suture, gather up my swabs and instruments, put the needles into a sharps bin, remove the green drapes and peel off my gloves. The midwife's scissor cut was expertly made and I've managed to close the perineal layers in the way I've been taught. Brenda's wound will heal up well. I help her out of the stirrups and make sure she's comfortable. Then I reassure her that it's all over and that everything's fine. 'Thank you, Doctor,' Brenda says. 'I hardly felt a thing. But now I'm so tired I'm going to have a sleep.'

I say goodbye and leave her to share her personal space with her new baby, then go back to bed and get some sleep before my pager goes off again. On this occasion, everything went smoothly. But things don't always go according to plan. In the next chapter, we'll look at those scary times when things go wrong.

6. Getting it wrong and putting it right

One night at Baragwanath Hospital in Soweto, I start operating on Jonas, a young man who has been stabbed in the neck. I haven't been at Bara very long. To say I'm anxious would be an understatement. Neck wounds are notorious. A combination of spasm in an artery's wall and a temporary blood clot often stop the initial bleeding, and at first the damage doesn't seem too serious. This comforting sense of security disappears abruptly when you dislodge the clot and a pulsating fountain of blood hits you in the face. Before you know where you are, torrential bleeding swamps your view. If a major vessel like the carotid artery has been damaged, blood under pressure forces its way into the surrounding tissues, distorting everything. Boundaries between anatomical structures become obliterated and you lose your bearings. But if arteries are bad, veins are worse. Make a hole in one of those – their walls are paper-thin, so it's perilously easy to do – and an ominous whooshing gives you a second's warning that a tidal wave of blood is about to blot everything out. It's one of the most terrifying things that can happen.

With Jonas I'm picking my way through a morass of

soggy tissue, trying to locate vital structures. As I probe and snip, I'm about to cut through some dreary-looking connective tissue. Something – I still don't know what – makes me stop and look again. I realize with a lurch that what I was about to divide is actually the internal jugular vein. This crucial vessel drains blood from the brain back to the heart, and cutting through it would be a disaster. A heart-stopping moment in every sense. I freeze, uncertain of what to do next. To gain time, I press hard with a swab and wait for my pulse to settle, thinking how close I just came to causing a catastrophe.

I try to summon my knowledge of neck anatomy. I should know it backwards. But I'm early in my surgical training and I haven't been operating solo for very long. The neck is scary territory at the best of times – even during a planned operation when you can see the tightly packed anatomy you've learned about from textbooks and in the dissecting room. But when someone has been stabbed, any certainty goes out of the window.

Flying solo

Head and neck anatomy is unbelievably complicated; I wasn't alone in finding it confusing. In my first year as a medical student, I went to see our family doctor for something and mentioned I'd just started at medical school. He pulled down a pristine copy of *Gray's Anatomy* from his bookshelf and handed it to me. 'Here,' he said, 'you might as well have this – I won't need it. I never could learn the names of those little buggers in the neck. Still have nightmares about them. Good luck.' Soon, I found out exactly what he meant.

Years later, when I was teaching anatomy to medical students, I became more familiar with those little buggers in the neck. We spent a whole term on the head and neck. At last, I understood the 'strap muscles' whose names seemed designed to confuse: sternohyoid, sternothyroid, omohyoid, thyrohyoid. I learned how the structures fitted into one another: the great arteries and veins taking blood to and from the brain; the nerves spreading out in all directions; the trachea taking air through the larynx to the lungs; and the treacherous oesophagus with its evil reputation as an unforgiving structure that was difficult to heal. Day after day, I guided groups of students through their dissections. By the end of that year, I had a pretty good idea about anatomy. I passed the primary exam for surgeons and felt smugly confident that those medical-school mists had dispersed. I'd memorized the names of all the little buggers and I knew exactly where to find them. At last, I knew it all. And it hadn't even been that difficult, really.

With Jonas on the operating table, I found out the difference between learning information and having knowledge. Anatomy in a living person is totally different from anatomy in a cadaver. I was way out of my depth, but there was no one to call on. I had to get on with it. I was flying solo and the stakes were real.

In this chapter we'll explore what happens when you're on the cusp between Apprentice and Journeyman. You've spent years on the early parts of the path I outlined in Chapter 1. Until now, you've been learning to do things in the way they're done by others. You've been wrapped in a protective blanket. The people you work with know you'll make mistakes, because of your inexperience and lack of skill. As an Apprentice, you are at first only too aware of how little you know (the 'conscious incompetence' I described in Chapter 3). Gradually, though, the technical difficulties start to recede. You're no longer having to use your full attention for everything, to concentrate so hard on what you're doing. You become more confident and you start to take things for granted. You are given licence to do more on your own. Eventually, you are on the verge of becoming independent, of moving into the Journeyman phase.

By this point you may think you know more than you actually do. You have become expert within the narrow compass of what your protected surroundings have allowed you to experience. Once those surroundings change, when you're out there on your own, you find you're up against challenges you didn't even know existed. Now you experience a different category of getting it wrong, one with serious consequences for all concerned. This is especially evident when the materials you work with are other people.

You can't help making mistakes – they're an inevitable part of becoming expert. When I started that operation on Jonas's neck I was beginning to take responsibility for my work, to lead operations on my own. But I was still wet behind the ears in terms of trauma surgery. Although I was gaining confidence, I didn't yet know how much I didn't know. All the experts I've worked with have similar stories of stopping just in time before something bad happens, of narrowly avoiding disaster.

Errors of this kind happen when you move from doing component tasks in someone else's workshop to taking responsibility for your work as a whole. That's the stage I'd reached when I was operating on Jonas. When you're at the limits of your competence and experience, but you have to carry on anyway, you're bound to make mistakes. Often, you notice in time and put it right. To improve, you have to expand the borders of your ability, and you'll only do that through work that stretches you. But sometimes bad things happen – work is damaged, people get hurt, your confidence is shattered.

Dealing with error involves interacting with people you may have disappointed in all kinds of ways. Fabrice the hairstylist describes these interactions in terms of psychological skills, as opposed to technical skills with scissors and comb. This chapter is about recognizing and responding when things are going wrong. No matter how many books you read, or how much advice people give you, you have to experience it for yourself. You have to learn to deal with that sick lurch when you realize you're on the verge of disaster. That's what happens when you go solo.

'Flying solo' is a hackneyed shorthand for doing something on your own. But sometimes it's literal. While I was becoming a surgeon in Soweto, I learned to fly. It was a crazy thing to do but I loved it.

Every day as I drove to and from the hospital, I passed a tiny airfield next to the road. A battered sign said 'Baragwanath Flying School'. One day, I went in. The flying school headquarters was a single-storey shack. One runway, no control tower, just a couple of tiny single-engine aeroplanes on the tarmac. It turned out that the school ran taster flights, where you could go up with an instructor for an hour to see if you liked it. I went up with Bill. A gruff, grizzled Afrikaner, he had been flying for decades and had seen it all. We took off in a two-seater, with me in the co-pilot's seat with its dual controls. Once we had gained some height, Bill pointed out the hospital below us and the skyline of Johannesburg in the distance. It was magical. Then he allowed me to fly the plane.

Of course, I wasn't really flying it – certainly not in the sense of taking any responsibility. But I was using the stick and the rudder, making the aircraft bank and turn; using my senses and learning about space and about other people. I had a glimpse of the mise en place of the cockpit and the other planes in the sky that we needed to avoid. Back on terra firma, I signed up for lessons on the spot.

The plane was a Cessna 152, one of the smallest you could get. It was like a second-hand car with wings, and its call sign was Kilo Sierra Lima (KSL). Over the next few months I came to know KSL extremely well. To begin with, all I did was 'circuits and bumps'. Bill and I spent hours taking off and landing, again and again, not stopping after we'd touched down but opening the throttle and taking off for another 'circuit'. I got to know that circuit by heart – a notional rectangle above the runway, each component with its technical name of crosswind leg, downwind leg, base leg and final approach. Time after time I went through the checklist procedures for taking off, gaining height, adjusting to the weather conditions, landing, then doing it all again. Crosswind landings. Flaps up, flaps down.

One day, after yet another set of take-offs and landings, Bill told me to stop. I thought I must have done something wrong and braced myself for a dressing-down. Instead, he got out of the cockpit and closed his door. 'I'll be in the school building,' he said. 'Let me know when you're back.' Before I'd realized quite what was happening, I'd taken off and was looking down at the flying school, this time on my own.

Everything changes when you're up there alone. All those lessons, that theory, those procedures become a blur. It's just you, and there's no Bill making tiny adjustments as you come in to land. But somehow things fell into place, I landed safely and brought KSL to a standstill. This moment occurs in the path of every expert. At a certain point, everybody has to stand on their own two feet.

After that, my confidence started to grow. I went out to the airfield on my own in the early mornings before work. I put in the hours I needed. I practised getting in and out of incipient spins and recovering from stalls. Eventually the day came for my flying test. The examiner put me through my paces. I showed I could take off on a short runway in a crosswind, navigate along a flight path, and make an emergency landing if the engine failed. I proudly received my Private Pilot Licence and couldn't wait to start using it.

Soon after that, I made a blunder that could have killed me and hundreds of others.

Recovering from error

Everyone makes errors. Nobody sets out to make them, but that's how life is and that's how we learn. So far in the book we've looked at practising your craft within a setting which protects you and has safeguards against too much harm. Fabrice started by shampooing, and Joshua began with pocket flaps. I didn't leap in by operating on stab wounds to the neck. I started with straightforward clinical procedures, like taking blood. As a medical student and a junior doctor, there were always people I could call on – though in the culture of the time I didn't unless I had no choice. But everyone knew I was learning and they made allowances. If I was really stuck I could call for help, and the only damage would be to my pride.

But there comes a point when you have to take direct responsibility for your work. You fetch up against the *consequences* of that work, especially when its focus is other people. You are having to make decisions in a world which no longer makes allowances for your mistakes. You chose to go there, and you have to deal with it.

Sometimes you find yourself out of your depth, your usual landmarks erased. Sometimes, as I discovered in that operation on Jonas's stabbed neck, you stop on the edge of disaster. But sometimes you don't stop, and bad things happen.

It's how you learn from your mistakes that counts. That's easy enough to say, but it's difficult to cope with when you damage someone else through your inexperience or inattention. Not all my own mistakes were medical. For one of my more spectacular blunders we'll go back to Baragwanath Flying School, where my first major error was nearly my last.

Soon after I got my pilot's licence, I took off in KSL on a short hop to Rand Airport. Rand was one of several large airports in Johannesburg but I'd never been there before. My flying school was so small it didn't have a control tower, and I wanted to practise flying to somewhere larger. My instructor Bill told me, 'You can't miss Rand Airport. Just turn left at the silver water tower soon after take-off and you'll see the runway ahead of you.'

I took off, saw the silver water tower and turned left. At first I couldn't spot the airport, so I kept going for a bit longer. Eventually I saw a sizeable runway. Although it was a little to one side of where I was expecting, I radioed Rand Airport tower, got clearance and landed. The runway seemed very long as I was taxiing along it, but it was only when I passed a row of jumbo jets and a sign saying 'Welcome to Johannesburg International Airport' that I realized I'd landed unannounced at one of the continent's busiest airports instead of the one I was aiming for. Soon after that my radio crackled into life, with a furious voice barking 'Kilo Sierra Lima, Kilo Sierra Lima, do you read me?'

I parked my little Cessna in front of the tower, then spent the next half hour in a most uncomfortable interview with the air traffic controller and his team. By sheer luck it had been a quiet afternoon, with no passenger aircraft scheduled to take off or land. If I'd come down in the path of an incoming airliner I could have caused a catastrophic crash, killing myself and a planeload of others.

The only reason I wasn't crucified was that the tower crew had relaxed their normal vigilance and hadn't noticed me coming until I'd actually landed. Red faces all round. Although the primary fault was mine, the safety net that should have picked up my mistake early had failed too. So after a severe dressing-down I was allowed to get back into KSL, much chastened, and fly back to Baragwanath airfield.

As soon as I landed, I told Bill what I had done. Bill was not known for his sensitivity and I braced myself for a tirade. But to my astonishment he burst into laughter, took me into a private room, produced a bottle from somewhere, poured us both a glass and started to tell me about the time he wrote off a twin-engine plane by forgetting to put down the undercarriage. More stories followed and I realized that, by making my mistake, I had moved one step nearer the centre of a community of practice. I'd joined the company of pilots who had made errors they didn't normally talk about; people who know that error is inevitable but who only tell you about theirs when you've made one yourself – just like surgeons.

Bill didn't minimize the seriousness of my mistake. It could have been horrendous, and it was sheer luck that I didn't cause a major disaster. But he realized that I needed to use that experience to become a better pilot, not let it make me lose my nerve so I never flew again.

Dissecting error

Although technically categorized as a 'near miss', my error with KSL was way beyond the 'normal' margin of error that beginners find themselves in. Nothing like it had ever happened at that airport – no aircraft would ever arrive at a large airport like that without making radio contact long before coming into view. Because my mistake was so egregious, it had never occurred to me or anyone else that it might even happen. The control tower team and I were both working within what we were expecting, and the unfamiliar floored us. I was focusing on my procedures for landing, without asking if I was at the right place. It was the aviation equivalent of doing a perfect operation on the wrong patient.

My near misses in surgery were of a different kind. These were caused by finding myself in unfamiliar terrain and not knowing what to do. When I was operating on Jonas, I found it impossible to recognize the usual landmarks. I'd operated on the neck before, but now the neck looked different.

Another night at Bara I was operating on a patient with penetrating chest and abdominal wounds. I didn't even know his name at the time, as he was almost dead from blood loss when he arrived. We had to take him straight to theatre. As I finished dealing with his abdominal injuries, his condition plummeted and I realized I had to go into his chest. The knife that stabbed him must have been a long one as there was bleeding from the great vessels near the heart. I hadn't seen much thoracic surgery, let alone done any, and yet again I was way outside my comfort zone. But there was no alternative, so I carried on.

Thoracic surgery is a specialized field and needs specialized instruments. After opening the chest, I found that blood was hosing from one of the large vessels to the lung. I could see where it was coming from, and I needed to stop it fast if my patient was to survive.

In this kind of emergency you can't take your eye off the site of injury, and your scrub nurse plays a vital role by putting what you need into your hand. On this occasion, the nurse with me hadn't done much thoracic surgery either. I asked for an angled clamp to control the bleeding, held out my hand and felt the instrument's handle hit my palm. I was just about to place it across the fragile vessel when I realized that, instead of the soft vascular clamp I was expecting, she had given me a bronchial clamp. This has murderous spikes in its jaws, designed to grasp the stiff cartilage of the air passages. It would have cut the delicate pulmonary vessels to shreds. To this day, I can feel the pounding of my heart as I realized what a narrow escape my patient and I had both just had.

My near misses in the operating theatre and in the air have similarities and differences. Thinking back to when I arrived unannounced at Johannesburg International Airport, I can identify several classic types of blunder. Landing at the wrong airport was an error through simple inexperience. The weather was fine; there was no obvious problem. I should have known better, but I didn't have the experience to recognize key signals and respond appropriately. I just hadn't learned enough. When I took off from Baragwanath airfield I was using my attentional capacity to fly the plane, talk on the radio and look out for the silver water tower. I didn't have a clear sense of where I was going, and I hadn't been there before. I took the advice of people who were more experienced than I was, people who assumed my knowledge was like theirs. For them, 'turn left at the silver water tower' told them all they needed to know. But what I needed to know was what to do *after* turning left. It didn't occur to me that there might be more than one airport in the vicinity. Though I'd studied the aerial charts until I was sick of them while I was swotting for my Private Pilot Licence, I hadn't made the connection.

On top of that, I was anxious. When I did see a runway, I was so relieved that I jumped to the conclusion that it was the right one, even though it wasn't exactly where I expected. Instead of questioning my assumptions, I over-focused on landing the plane. This ties in with Daniel Kahneman's System 1 and System 2 thinking. In my case, I worked according to System 1 – the fast, automatic way – when I should have been using System 2, the painstaking effortful approach which analyses factors systematically.

It is frighteningly easy to make assumptions. In surgical training you spend a long time learning anatomy, mostly from textbooks. This is highly detailed knowledge and it provides a reassuring sense of certainty. But that certainty can be illusory. You think in terms of 'a gastrectomy' (removing the stomach) – of descriptions you have seen in books and other patients you have been involved with. But you can't know what *this* patient's stomach will be like until you see it for yourself.

In Chapter 4 I described the need to look, really look, at what's in front of you, rather than seeing what you expect to find. As my experience in the air showed me, when you're feeling vulnerable – uncertain, out of your depth, tired, and all the other things the books don't mention – this is the very time when you need to take note of warning signs and not just plough on. Luckily, that's what I did with Jonas as I was about to divide his internal jugular vein. But sometimes you are forced out of your comfort zone because the circumstances are beyond your control. You find yourself in territory you wouldn't have chosen and you cannot avoid. If you're lucky you can call for help, but often you just have to deal with it.

Error has a bad name, but it's both important and unavoidable. The challenge is not to eliminate it but to minimize the damage it causes. There's a difference between 'bad error' (those harmful mistakes that should have been avoided) and 'honourable error' (when you try something and it doesn't work). There's no shame in honourable error. On the contrary, it's how people move forward. Error then becomes something to learn from, something to be experienced, corrected and reshaped, rather than avoided altogether. Nobody sets out to make mistakes, but learning from error is an essential part of becoming expert. It's how you improve. Error and failure are not the same.

The danger of making assumptions

At around the time I was landing at the wrong airport, Fabrice the hairstylist was starting with his last client of the day in the salon where he was completing his training.

The pressure was on to finish quickly so that the salon could close on time. By now Fabrice had gained a lot of technical skill. He was expert with scissors and comb, with handling different kinds of hair. After years of apprenticeship he hardly had to think about what he was doing, and he could keep up a conversation on autopilot while he worked.

On this occasion, his client was a middle-aged woman with shortish hair. Partway through, he suddenly realized that he'd cut the hair on her crown too short. Hairstylists have a saying, 'When it's too short, it's too late'; that day, Fabrice had that sinking feeling I'd experienced many times in the operating theatre.

To an outsider, hairstyling seems to be about technique, about shaping and snipping. In fact, the most important part is design. Everyone's hair grows differently and those growth patterns are crucial, especially on the crown. If you get that wrong you'll create something that may look reasonable at first but quickly becomes distorted as the hair grows. It's especially challenging with shorter hair, where even a millimetre can make a huge difference.

Fabrice had made an unforced error and now he had to handle it. Building on the relationship he had developed with this client over previous visits, he was straightforward. 'I've made it a little shorter than we planned,' he said, 'and perhaps I misjudged the growth pattern. In two weeks' time it should be fine, but today it will look a bit shorter than you expected. Will you be OK with that?' The client wasn't pleased, but she accepted Fabrice's explanation. The next time she made an appointment she even insisted on being styled by him again.

Fabrice made that mistake through overconfidence. Relying on the techniques he was beginning to master, he overlooked the need to check and recheck whether he was doing the right thing. Later, he discovered that all stylists make errors of this kind, even when they are extremely experienced. Fabrice had become part of a community of stylists who had made errors. Even the most famous are not immune. The fashion designer Mary Quant once described having her hair cut by the iconic stylist Vidal Sassoon in the 1960s. 'One night,' Quant recalled, '[he] was cutting my hair to promote his new five-point geometric bob, in the presence of various Press photographers. Spurred on by the vast audience, he went whap! – and cut my ear. Just the fat bit – and nothing bleeds more.'

Joshua the tailor made mistakes at this stage of his career too. When he'd just finished his second apprenticeship and was starting to work as a qualified tailor, he deliberately sought out challenging customers in order to gain experience. One of these was a man who suffered a physical disability and had an unusual body shape. He and Joshua decided on a design for his suit, then Joshua began a series of fittings. By the third fitting he discovered that things were getting worse, not better.

Joshua was skilled in making suits for average-looking people, but he didn't yet have the experience to deal with outliers. He realized that he'd never be able to make the successful suit he had in mind by tinkering with what he'd created so far. His fundamental design, based on a man of more usual proportions, was an error. Bravely, he decided to scrap what he'd done, go back to the beginning and start again from scratch. He was able to use what he'd learned from that false start to come up with a different design. In the end, the suit was a success, and the customer was delighted. But Joshua had to recognize when his situation needed a radical rethink rather than fiddling. He'd had to write off everything he had done so far – the materials, the work of the making tailors, his time and his customer's time – and that took guts. But his priority was to do the best work possible, and he could only do that by starting again. So Joshua moved out of the frame he had been working in – the approaches he'd been taught and the assumptions he'd grown used to – and set up a different one. This is difficult to do, but it's an essential part of improving. That ability to change frames is a marker of becoming expert.

I experienced something similar after I'd been a GP for several years. One of my patients came to see me because she was tired. Bethany was in her forties, with a family and a busy career. There was nothing specific in her history apart from some indigestion. I arranged a blood test which confirmed that she was anaemic, so the next step was to find out why. I had a niggling worry that there might be something more serious going on, as I'd known Bethany for years and she didn't look quite right. So, because of the indigestion, I referred her to a gastroenterologist. He arranged various tests including an endoscopy (passing a flexible tube into the stomach and another into the rectum), and all the results came back normal. He reassured Bethany that nothing was wrong. But a few months later she saw me again because her tiredness was getting worse.

Although the hospital consultant had given her the green light, I realized that was only from his perspective as a specialist. When he said there was nothing wrong, he meant nothing wrong with her digestive system – not that there was nothing wrong at all. As a GP, my job was to step back and think whether we'd been asking the right questions. Maybe her problem was not with her digestive system but another part of her body altogether.

In the end, it turned out that Bethany had an early cancer of the uterus. Luckily, we caught it in time and she was fine, but I could easily have missed it. It is surprisingly easy to start down a path from the initial framing of a problem and stay within that set of assumptions. I had to learn to stop, rewind and think again – to check whether I was treating the right problem.

I'm sure we've all made errors through assumption, treating a symptom rather than its cause. When a light goes out in the house, your immediate response is to change the bulb. But when that bulb blows too, you have to look for a different explanation. It happened with the battered old Morris Minor van I used to drive as a student. One day it coughed and died by the side of the road. The petrol gauge said 'Full', so I knew that couldn't be the problem. I called the roadside rescue service and the first thing the mechanic did was pour in some petrol from a can. The car started without a murmur and I felt like a complete idiot. It turned out that my petrol gauge was faulty and had stuck on 'Full'.

Mistaking the frame

If you make a textbook landing at the wrong airport or perfectly execute an unsuitable hairstyle, your error is not a failure of technique. It's a failure to perceive the bigger picture. Becoming expert means you have to combine knowledge and skill with an understanding of the whole context. You have to be vigilant for what is happening around the edges of your situation, not just at the centre.

By this stage, you're on the verge of becoming a Journeyman, of working independently. Error has different consequences and implications from when you were an Apprentice. Errors now may affect the work itself, your colleagues, or others such as patients or passengers. And for every full-blown error there will be lots of near misses. Some of these will be blameworthy, others not. But part of becoming expert is developing resilience, carrying on without either trivializing errors or allowing them to destroy you. As Samuel Beckett tersely put it: 'Ever tried. Ever failed. No matter. Try again. Fail again. Fail better.'

This requires self-awareness and insight. Back in the world of medicine, Renée Fox – in her 1957 book *Training for Uncertainty* – identifies three types of uncertainty. 'The first results from incomplete or imperfect mastery of available knowledge,' she writes. 'The second depends upon limitations in current medical knowledge . . . The third source of uncertainty derives from the first two. This consists of difficulty in distinguishing between personal ignorance or ineptitude and the limitations of present medical knowledge.' While Fox was focused on medicine, this holds true in all fields of expertise: it's hard to know what you don't know.

Often it's not because people don't know enough that they make errors, but because for some reason they do the wrong thing. No matter how many times someone tells you to save your project on the computer, sooner or later you don't bother and a day's work is lost. However often your boss warns you not to over-tighten a nut on an engine you're working on, one day you go too far and shear it off. This kind of error is how you develop an embodied understanding of the material world and what it feels like to interact with it. This is how you learn to recognize limits, to know when materials or people are on the verge of collapse. It's only by shearing off a nut that you stock your internal library with 'tight' and 'over-tight'. It's a horrible feeling, but it happens to us all.

It happened to me when I was building my harpsichord. By that time, it was over ten years since my debacle at Johannesburg Airport and I was back in the

UK. After six months, the end was in sight. I'd finished the basic assembly, put the keyboard into position and shaped the hundreds of jacks for the strings. I was on to the 'voicing', scraping and shaping the plectra to give the instrument its touch and tone.

The art of voicing is to shave each plectrum with a scalpel so that its volume and tone matches the other notes. Once you've learned to use the scalpel without slicing your thumb off, you work on each plectrum in turn. This is a challenge. Take off too little and the sound is harsh and aggressive. Take off too much and it becomes barely audible. A fraction further and the plectrum snaps. The process gets more difficult as you go on, because the heavier bass strings need firmer plectra than the lightweight treble ones. Voicing harpsichord plectra is working with thin materials on the verge of collapse. Like Duncan Hooson and his pottery vases, the line between too little and too much is very fine.

Finally, after months of work, my harpsichord was finished. Every note worked, the voicing sounded reasonable and I couldn't wait to play it. But first I had to get it out of the tiny bedroom where I'd built it, allowing my youngest daughter to return. When it was in a larger room, I discovered to my horror that I could hardly hear it. The sound was completely lost: I had shaved all the plectra too far. In what I later learned was a classic beginner's blunder, I had voiced it for the room where I was making it, not the room where it would be played. In the words of Fabrice and the hairstylists, when it's too short, it's too late. You can't put it back if you remove too much. All you can do is start again. I had to remove every one of those two hundred plectra and go through the whole painful process again. I was furious with myself.

Here were several problems. I'd never built a harpsichord before, so I had no idea of the stages which lay ahead of me or what it should sound like. I was building the instrument in isolation, away from anybody who could help, so I wasn't part of a community of practice. I was trying to interpret instructions written by somebody who was already expert and knew what the final outcome should be. Such instructions assume prior knowledge, which in my case I did not have. And because I'd never played a harpsichord, I didn't really know what mine should sound like or how it should feel. I had few coordinates when plotting my path through making that instrument, and no clear idea of where I was heading.

Collective error and collusion

My error in voicing the harpsichord was mine alone, caused by my inexperience and an inability to understand the bigger picture. But unlike mistakes in an individual's workshop, errors in surgery are seldom caused by one person alone. Sometimes they happen by default, by inaction or by a collective reluctance to intervene. Sometimes they are difficult to explain afterwards.

I experienced this at first hand during one of my hospital attachments – a cardiac surgery unit where the atmosphere was toxic. For some reason, the consultants seemed to be at war with one another. As a registrar (a surgeon in training), I felt the brunt of this hostility. After heart surgery, patients go to the intensive care unit (ICU) to recover. At any time, the ICU would contain patients for each of the consultants I worked for. One of my jobs was to make sure these patients were stable, and to adjust the intravenous drugs that supported their hearts after the operation. Every four hours there would be an ICU ward round. The consultant surgeons would take it in turns to lead the round and give instructions. Each countermanded the orders of the one before, for no good reason that I could see except to impose their authority. It was a horrible place to work.

Part of my job involved assisting at open heart operations, where patients with aortic or mitral valve disease would be put onto a cardiopulmonary bypass (heart–lung machine), so that their heart could be stopped, the faulty valve cut out and an artificial one put in. Although the operation was routine and generally safe, it was important to minimize how long the patient remained on bypass, as it could lead to brain damage and other complications.

Replacement valves at that time consisted of a silastic ball within a metal cage. As the heart contracts, the ball moves forward into the cage and allows the blood to flow. As the heart relaxes, the ball falls back and blocks the flow. The cage was surrounded by a fabric ring, which allowed the new valve to be securely sewn in with a watertight join.

One day, I was the second assistant in a valve replacement performed by a senior consultant. The first assistant was an experienced registrar who was specializing in cardiac surgery, and the rest of the team (scrub nurse, runners, pump technician and many others) had done this procedure countless times. I'd only ever seen a couple of valve replacements.

Once the patient was on bypass and the heart had been stopped, the consultant swiftly excised the diseased valve. Then he began the painstaking process of sewing in the new one. As usual, he started by inserting a circle of long sutures, each taking a firm bite through the residual rim of the diseased valve before passing through the fabric ring of the replacement. He would slide the new valve down these threads until it was snugly seated in the heart, then tie the sutures.

While this was happening, I got an uncomfortable feeling. I tried to visualize what this new valve would look like once it was in the heart, thinking which way the silastic ball would move in its cage. It didn't seem right and I couldn't imagine how the blood would flow through it in the proper direction. I almost wondered if I should say something, but it seemed unimaginable that this highly experienced surgeon could put in a valve the wrong way round. Anyway, surely the other (also highly experienced) members of the team would shout if there was a problem. So I said nothing. I carried on holding my retractor while the surgeon slid the valve into position and tied all the sutures. His first assistant cut each of the excess threads, leaving a tiny knot.

Suddenly the surgeon realized what had happened. All the usual theatre noises stopped and there was a profound silence. First, very quietly, he said, 'Fuck.' Then: 'Sister, I'll need to remove the valve and put it in again.' Everyone knew how serious this was, as the additional time would take the patient into the danger zone for being on bypass. Nobody said a word as he cut all the stitches, removed the valve and went through the whole process a second time. Afterwards, I never heard anybody allude to it. It was as if it had never happened. Luckily, the patient was fine, but it was a mistake which could have had devastating consequences.

Thinking back over that experience, I can understand it from the surgeon's perspective. One cause of error is the narrowing of attention that comes with stressful, high-stakes work. Experts depend on the ability to focus on what they are doing and push away distractions. By zooming in on the work at hand, they give it their undivided attention. But this risks over-focusing on one part of the picture, blunting their awareness of what's happening all around. It is easy to imagine becoming so absorbed in a task like putting in a heart valve that wider questions about whether it's the right way round might become lost. You could become preoccupied by the challenges of sewing brittle tissue, adjusting suture tension to ensure a leak-proof fit, and completing the task with swift efficiency. As I learned the hard way in Johannesburg in my little Cessna, and again when voicing my harpsichord back in the UK, it's all too easy to lose sight of the big picture when you're struggling with the details.

The bigger question is about that surgical team. To this day I cannot understand why nobody said anything. Many people must have known – the first assistant certainly, the scrub nurse too, and most likely others in the room. Probably, it was a combination of an unwillingness to challenge authority, a fear of ridicule by talking out of turn, and a potentially lethal dash of *Schadenfreude* within a workplace that was based on competition between ambitious professionals rather than collaboration for the benefit of patients. Even I'd had an inkling but was too afraid to speak up. At that stage I was a peripheral participant in a community of practice whose ways I hadn't become familiar with, and I allowed myself to collude in a shared silence.

Patient safety is a major issue worldwide. Medicine and surgery have learned a lot from aviation, especially in terms of authority within the cockpit. This problem of collusive silence is well known in hierarchical systems. Responding to a series of catastrophic accidents over many years, often caused by communication failure, aviation has empowered everyone to have a voice and to feel comfortable in stating the obvious. Current airline practice expects every member of the team to speak out if they notice anything amiss – and they do. I often thought about my experience with the heart valve in the years that followed, as evidence mounted that medical errors are seldom the fault of one person. I kept wondering why I hadn't spoken up.

The enormous body of literature on error shows that few disasters are caused by individual incompetence, inattention or sheer bad luck. But case after case also demonstrates how individuals are blamed for wider issues within organizations and systems. This continues to happen with medical errors, and high-profile examples such as the paediatrician Dr Hadiza Bawa-Garba, under whose care a child died, have exposed fault lines in the way that medical and other professions deal with harm. Experts such as James Reason, Don Berwick, Charles Vincent and Atul Gawande have explored the assumptions we make, the actions we take and the difficulties we have in acknowledging and learning from error. Their insights fit with research from safety-critical industries such as aviation, offshore oil drilling and nuclear power.

James Reason is well known for his 'Swiss cheese' model of error. He has pointed out that weaknesses in a system are like holes in a slice of Emmental. If several slices line up, they allow an error to pass through and cause disaster. That's what happened when I landed unannounced in KSL at Johannesburg airport: I flew along the lined-up holes in the Swiss cheese. I was inexperienced, the control tower team were inattentive, the system's level of alertness was low. By good fortune, there wasn't an airliner coming through those same holes in the cheese towards me. But it was a close shave. I hope that the control tower team learned as much as I did.

Experts and error

So what is the relationship between error and learning? Error can have a devastating effect on you and your work, even if nobody gets killed or injured. When you make a mistake, it's easy to believe that you have failed as a person and allow it to shatter your self-belief. Somehow you have to distinguish between the consequences of error for your work and its impact upon you. How you navigate this determines whether you frame error as a constructive process, by which you mature and progress, or a destructive one which demolishes your confidence. Musicians and managing directors alike will talk about preparation, performance and recovery as resilience: the ability to survive when things go wrong and to make something positive of the experience. Yet despite its power to teach us, error in many settings remains a dirty word.

Sometimes mistakes happen through ignorance, inattention or hubris. If that's the case, you need to acknowledge those unappealing aspects of yourself and head off repetitions. (I certainly never landed a plane at the wrong airport again.) At other times, error is just a painful part of becoming expert. Of course, the consequences of error depend on your field of expertise. There is an old truism that nobody dies if you play a wrong note on the concert platform, whereas if you're performing a surgical operation or flying an aeroplane, error can literally be fatal. That's true when you focus on those who experience the error – the audience, patients or passengers. But the effect of error can be devastating for those making it too. If playing a wrong note early in a pianist's career leads to debilitating stage fright, they can get stuck in their path to becoming expert. It is only if you can learn from error and build up resilience that you can progress to the later stages.

Back in the Bara operating theatre with Jonas, I wait for my heart to stop pounding. I have to put aside the nightmare of what could have happened if I'd snipped that grey squidgy structure that turned out to be his internal jugular vein. I'd been working with too much speed and I'd made assumptions. Fighting down a sense of panic, I force myself to be systematic, to take things slowly and examine every structure I encounter. Gradually, the knowledge from textbooks and the dissecting room reasserts itself and I start to make sense of the landscape of Jonas's injured neck, and all those little buggers I'd spent so long memorizing. I recognize some familiar structures and get back on track. I realize that the operation may be difficult but it's not beyond the boundaries of my skill. I may be butting up against my limits, but as long as I'm strict with myself and maintain focus, I can do it.

Eventually I find where the blood is coming from. I control the bleeding with vascular clamps and close the hole with tiny stitches. I take the clamps off and breathe a sigh of relief when the operative field stays dry. Finally, I'm able to close the wound and send Jonas to the recovery bay. Every time I see Jonas on the ward after that, I think what a narrow escape we both had. I'm relieved he's getting better but I have a queasy feeling that my inexperience put me a hair's breadth from making a bad situation infinitely worse. But that comes with the territory of flying solo.

So, error is something that happens to us all. But there is a distinction between the errors we make through inexperience, the ones we make through sloppiness or inattention, and those 'honourable errors' that come from trying things out and finding they don't work. If you are going to improve, you have to venture out from the safety of the workshop or studio into the real world, and that involves getting things wrong. Now the errors you make have consequences, both for you and for other people. Part of becoming expert is developing resilience, finding ways of coping that neither minimize the impact of your actions nor damage your confidence beyond repair.

You are now poised at the threshold between the sheltered world of the Apprentice and the harsher milieu of the independent practitioner, the Journeyman. We've already seen some of the bad things that can happen, the near misses and narrow squeaks. The next chapters explore the internal shifts that have to take place as you push yourself out there and develop the individuality that defines the expert you are going to become. At the time it seems like magic. And, in a sense, it is.

APPRENTICE   JOURNEYMAN   MASTER

PASSING
IT ON

DOING
TIME

'IT'S NOT
ABOUT YOU'

USING YOUR
SENSES

DEVELOPING
VOICE

SPACE AND
OTHER PEOPLE

7. 'It's not about you'

It's 1990 and I'm in my GP consulting room in Trowbridge. I've only seen Sarah a couple of times before
when she makes an appointment just after Christmas. I
haven't been in general practice for very long and I'm
keen to make my mark. I'm proud of my medical knowledge and I want to show it off.

Sarah often feels rather low, she tells me, especially in
the winter when the nights close in. This time she's
complaining of a spot of indigestion too. She thinks it's
because she's had a big family Christmas with her children and grandchildren, and they've all overdone it a bit.
Her appetite's been poor and she doesn't feel right,
though she can't put her finger on why. A few days ago
her husband said he thought the whites of her eyes
looked slightly yellow, but she thinks that's just a trick of
the light.

Looking at Sarah, I think her husband may be right
and I start to get an uneasy feeling. Jaundice is a worrying sign. After a few more questions, I ask her to lie on
my examination couch and I check her physically. As
soon as I put my hand on her abdomen ('palpating' it, to
use the technical term) I know that something's wrong.
As she breathes in and out I can feel the edge of her

liver; it's hard and irregular. All my surgical instincts kick in and I realize she has something serious, probably cancer.

In a clinical sense, I'm pleased to have recognized the problem. As a surgeon I've treated lots of patients with symptoms like Sarah's and I know what to do. She'll need blood tests, X-rays and scans, urgent referral to a specialist and then probably a major operation – the kind of operation I used to perform myself.

After I've examined Sarah and we're sitting at my desk, she asks me what I think the matter is. I'm on the brink of telling her, outlining the steps that lie ahead and at the same time letting her know what an acute diagnostician I am.

But then I remember it's not about me, it's about Sarah. I'm not showing off my knowledge on a ward round; I'm in a room with another person, trying to work out how to tell her she could be seriously ill. She's not interested in all the work I've done to get here, or the exams I've passed along the way. At this moment it's irrelevant. My knowledge only counts for anything if I can channel it into doing the right thing for Sarah. It's not about *what* I need to tell her, but *how*.

Something warns me not to go too fast. Instead of saying what I think the problem is, I ask her, 'What do *you* think might be wrong?' She looks at me for a long moment. Neither of us says a word.

The magic of care

This chapter explores the crucial transition 'from you to them'. We'll see how experts shift their focus from themselves to the people their work is for. At the heart of this lies *purpose*. Your purpose is why you're working to become an expert in the first place.

This shift from you to them is an internal process, and it often goes unnoticed. It doesn't always coincide with other aspects of development, with the transition from Apprentice to Journeyman and from supervised to independent practice. It's a shift which is challenging to spot. In some people, it's there from the outset. In others, it doesn't seem to happen at all. Yet this shift of emphasis is central to becoming an expert.

We're now in the second phase of the path to becoming expert. Now, you're applying what you've learned as an Apprentice to problems in the real world. You're no longer a protected trainee – you're taking responsibility for the impact of your work on other people. You've spent years doing time, you've become skilled at working with your tools and materials, and you're adept at navigating other people's personal space. You've been flying solo and you've had near misses. You've made mistakes and you've recovered. But all of this has been focused on you. It's been about *your* development, *your* skills, *your* mistakes. Now you have to switch your focus to other people.

I'll start by looking at an unusual kind of expert performance – magic. The seeming juxtaposition of serious illness and an entertaining magic show may strike a jarring note, but as I'll explain, there are powerful similarities between these apparently unconnected ways of being expert. They both rely on high levels of specialist knowledge and technical skill, and they both depend on caring for another person's experience.

Richard McDougall comes to your table at a function. You're with some friends and you're not expecting anyone else to join you. He asks if you'd like to see some magic. You say yes, and for the next few minutes you're spellbound by the extraordinary tricks he performs. Coins and cards develop a life of their own, defying the laws of nature. Things appear, hover in mid-air, then vanish. After a few minutes, he smiles at you all, says goodbye and leaves. It seems effortless, and somehow the experience wasn't weird or awkward. Richard hasn't intruded on your dinner; he's enriched it. He hasn't been showing off, he's brought something new to your table. He became part of your group, and joined your conversation. What has he done and how has he done it? What, in essence, is magic? When I asked Richard this, he said, 'You have to realize that magic isn't about you [the performer]. It's about them [the audience].'

Richard's magic is not about dexterity or skill, although he is extremely dextrous and highly skilled. His magic is about how he makes you feel. When learning to become a close-up magician, Richard spent years practising sleight-of-hand tricks. But sleight-of-hand tricks in themselves aren't magic. Magic needs an audience and that audience has to believe, just for a moment, that something impossible has really happened. For Richard, the crux came when he realized that it was the audience's experience that mattered, not his. When he performs, he's not just focusing on what he does, but on how it lands with those who see it. His observational faculties are highly tuned. He reads and responds to tiny signals in his audience that they're not even aware of.

Becoming expert requires you to focus on the people who experience your work – thinking from their perspective and not just your own. Alongside this shift comes a growing confidence in your own personality, and your identity as an expert. You have to subordinate yourself while also developing your uniqueness. It can be a difficult circle to square, and these two changes can pull in opposite directions. We'll explore that tension in the next chapter. But for now, we'll stay with the transition from you to them.

By the time I met Richard I'd become an academic. But talking to him took me back to my surgical career. When I was focusing on the skills of surgery, Richard was spending years working with cards and coins. We both became obsessed by the skills of our craft.

I loved operating. Most surgeons do. I revelled in the physicality of it, the sensation of working with living tissue. I found a satisfaction which was almost addictive.

Incising, exposing, dissecting, removing and re-joining; opening an abdomen, mobilizing a colon, displaying a ureter, resecting an injured segment of intestine or creating an elegant anastomosis. Even closing the skin with economy and grace could be deeply satisfying. I enjoyed becoming a craftsman with living human tissue. For a long time, my focus was on myself, on the skills I was developing. But I was operating on real people. I had to keep in mind why I was doing surgery, and who I was doing it for.

Over the course of my career, I've known of clinicians who put their keenness to intervene above their patients' best interests. Driven by an urge to 'cut', as that kind of surgeon might put it, they would rush to operate. Sometimes they allowed that to skew their judgement. Surgeons like this might carry out procedures that didn't really need to be done, or were beyond their experience. Sometimes they would get into difficulties, and needless harm would result. Operating became more about them than their patients. Their priorities were distorted, and things were out of balance.

For work to be expert, it must have a wider aim. Becoming expert takes years of dedicated effort; you need to have a good reason for doing it. Of course, there's personal satisfaction in being able to make, create and design. There's a reward in doing anything well for its own sake. But becoming expert is about something grander than that: it's doing something *for* other people. A crucial element is *care*; you have a responsibility of care for whoever or whatever you're working with. It could be clay or silver, Renaissance statues or living human beings – whatever the medium, you must respect it and look after it.

This is not a linear progression, with a clear transition from you to them. There isn't one particular moment when your focus moves from your own skills to other people's needs. It's a gradual process, with blurry edges. Whether you're a clinician or a magician, what actually happens is that you start performing before you've become fully confident. You're out there in front of an audience – doing magic, playing an instrument or leading an operation. You're scared stiff that you'll drop a card, forget your lines, damage a vital structure or just look like an idiot. That's the space in which technical mastery is honed.

But how can you ensure that the seductiveness of technical mastery doesn't override judgement, care and the wisdom to leave well alone? How can you ensure that you don't over-focus on yourself and lose sight of the reason you're there in the first place? These questions were going through my mind in my GP consulting room with Sarah, my patient with jaundice.

So I asked her to tell me more about what was going on. It turned out there was a lot happening in her life. Her son's marriage was looking rocky, and he was starting to drink again. One of her grandchildren was causing problems; she thought he might be being bullied at school, but he wouldn't talk about it. They were retrenching staff at the factory where she had worked for decades, and things were looking precarious financially. The last thing she could afford was to be ill.

The reality of Sarah's health didn't seem to be uppermost in her mind. Unlike me, she wasn't thinking about tests and operations. She was thinking about how to handle all those things going on in her family, and she had come to me because her tiredness was getting in the way. I was pretty sure that she'd got something serious, and the sooner I referred her for specialist treatment the better. But doing so might worsen the problems she was most worried about.

I needed Sarah to recognize the seriousness of her symptoms while balancing them against the other things that were happening in her life. Then I could help her work out what to do. Doctors, like all other experts, are there to identify problems and help solve them. But being a *good* doctor is not as simple as sending someone off for tests the moment you think there's something wrong.

Good judgement

I didn't even realize the need for a shift from myself to others until I'd been studying medicine for a long time. For many years, I was the centre of my medical world. Throughout my early career, I was being assessed on how much I knew. I was struggling to memorize facts, learn how to examine patients and develop procedural skills. I used the way I treated patients as proof to my colleagues and assessors that I knew my stuff. As I developed, I wanted to use these facts and techniques that had taken so long to learn.

When I was a trauma surgeon in Africa, my focus was learning to operate. When I took patients into theatre, their personalities almost disappeared. Often they had arrived at the hospital unconscious, so I hadn't got to know them before their surgery began. On the operating table, when they were under anaesthetic, I was forced to concentrate on their bodies. Each operation was a technical challenge, and I was developing my skills as a craftsman with human tissue. Even when my patients started to recover after surgery, I didn't have time to get to know them properly because I was so busy dealing with more patients.

At that time, I was thinking about how I could become more proficient and be allowed to take on more responsibility. I wanted to do more ambitious procedures, undertake trickier operations. I was absorbed in the *how* of surgery more than the *why*. Because my focus was on myself, I didn't think much about clinical judgement.

Good judgement is complex and can be difficult to recognize. When I was a junior member in a surgical team, it was my bosses who made the decision to operate. My focus was the operation. I wanted to 'assist' in theatre, then operate myself – I watched what my bosses did, and gradually they let me do things. During all those hours holding retractors, performing parts of operations and finally whole procedures under supervision, I was learning *how* to operate. But someone else had decided whether to operate, and what operation to do. Someone else was monitoring the wider situation. If something went wrong, they were there to take over and bail me out. At that stage, my ability to perform outstripped my experience and judgement. I was only seeing part of the landscape – each patient as a body, not a person.

Yet judging whether to operate and what operation to do can be the biggest challenge. One of my consultants when I was a surgical trainee told me, 'A surgeon knows how to operate; a good surgeon knows when to operate; a really good surgeon knows when not to operate.' The latter requires judgement and restraint. Your duty of care must override your wish to intervene. By the time I was leading trauma teams at Bara, I had to make those judgements for myself.

Joshua the tailor was learning something similar at this stage in his career. Joshua had spent four years learning to be a making tailor. Then he set out to become a cutting tailor. When he began this second apprenticeship, he had to learn a new set of skills. As a making tailor, his focus had been on himself and the techniques he was trying to master. That's when he was struggling to make pocket flaps and buttonholes; he spent years doing boring repetitive tasks of no apparent value at the time. By the end of that apprenticeship, he had mastered the technical aspects of his craft and become a skilled professional jacket-maker. Like me, his focus had been on his own skills.

As a customer or client ordering a bespoke suit, you never see making tailors and they don't see you, any more than a patient sees what goes on behind the scenes in an operating theatre. But a cutting tailor spends much of their time with customers. During a fitting, Joshua seems utterly at ease and unhurried, whatever else is going on in his life. The outside world fades away as he talks about this or that. Yet whether he's chatting about cricket or textile patterns, his conversation isn't just padding. It's how he builds relationships. He makes it clear to each client that they have his undivided attention. During a first visit he may show some sample books, registering the tiny cues that show what cloth that person likes and when they are just being polite. Like Richard the magician with his audience, Joshua is reading his client acutely. All the time, he's watching, thinking and taking mental notes. He's storing up those fine-grained observations to call upon later.

During each fitting Joshua walks round his customer, making occasional chalk marks on the embryonic jacket. Sometimes he starts to dismantle it there and then – 'ripping the jacket down', as tailors call this process – by snipping the tacking stitches which hold collar or sleeve in place, and pulling the elements apart so they can be reassembled with adjustments at the next fitting. This emphasizes to the client that Joshua is making that suit just for them – their body, their needs and their way of life. The garment reflects Joshua's understanding of *why* that person has come to have a suit or jacket made in the first place.

This is uncannily like being a doctor. First you listen, then you speak. When I became a GP, I moved from medicine's equivalent of a making tailor to that of a cutting tailor. The dexterity skills I had worked so hard to acquire moved into the background. It was no longer the operating theatre that defined me, but my consulting room instead.

Learning from the elbows up

It was magicians who made me recognize the shift from you to them. By that time, I'd made that shift myself, though I hadn't thought of it in those terms. For a magician, though, the shift is very obvious. Although the stakes in medicine are in a different league, magicians and clinicians both have an audience. Without an audience, there may be dexterity and skill, but there's no magic, no medicine. To succeed, you have to bring your audience with you.

By the time I first met Richard, I was at Imperial College London, running a master's programme in surgical education. Richard is one of the UK's leading close-up magicians, with awards galore. He's a member of the Inner Magic Circle (Gold Star) and a former World

Open Champion for close-up magic. He has given shows for the Queen and the Prince of Wales, and he performs around the world. Watching him work is uncanny. Of course the tricks that he does are impressive. Like all magicians at his level, he is a master of the apparently impossible. But even more remarkable is how he manages an audience, his ability to read people. This is a skill he's perfected over decades.

As a magician, Richard told me, your audience – whether it's of one or a thousand – needs to believe you are doing something impossible. During his early years, Richard set out to learn how to engage the people watching him; to capture and manage their attention. 'Magic isn't just about giving the wrong information,' he said. 'What magicians are very good at is making the unimportant seem incredibly important – and what's absolutely critical, very unimportant.'

Richard started learning magic at the age of six. When he was eight he 'retired', as he put it. A couple of years later he came out of retirement and got back to it in earnest. He began with the skills of physical manipulation, working with coins, cards and cups. Richard calls that 'learning from the elbows down'.

When Richard was learning it was all from books, but now there are videos online that allow you to copy an expert. Lots of beginners become very good at this. But however dextrous you are, moves are just moves unless there is an audience. There is no magic unless someone is watching. The *experience* of magic is jointly constituted.

That happens 'from the elbows up', and that's where Richard's real mastery lies.

When Richard performs, he creates a space where he engages with his audience. He uses his personality and charm to direct the audience's attention where he wants it. That establishes a place that is very close to where the audience is looking but which they are unaware of. As a magician, you have to understand how to move the spotlight of attention, to recognize where your audience is looking, and to make use of those spots of perceptual blindness as you perform a trick.

'It's like boxing,' Richard told me. 'Some positions suggest attack, others suggest defence. A boxer will feint, looking as if he's going to throw a punch. He'll create a space, then come in with the other hand. A magician does that too. You're creating a moment in an audience's mind where they think, "Something's about to happen, I've really got to watch this." But perhaps nothing happens, so they relax. And when their radar is lowered a little bit, that's when you can do something. Then you raise their attention again. These waves of attention and inattention that a magician learns to create are what allows him to make the technical moves imperceptible. It's not purely dexterity, there's a lot more going on.'

So how did Richard become the expert performer he is? He started with doing time. He cut his teeth in London's first 'magic restaurant', decades ago. He performed there at tables five days a week, with a thirteen-hour stretch on Saturdays. At that point he had mastered the dexterity, the 'tricks'. He had become an expert from the elbows down. But already that side of things was becoming repetitive and tedious, doing the same thing night after night.

He could have started to freewheel, relying on the well-worn skills he had mastered. Instead, he focused on becoming equally expert from the elbows up – on becoming an expert performer. He set himself challenges, like how to use body language to get a cocky young executive to sit back and relax, or make a powerful CEO lean forward and take notice. He could have spent his time developing fancier tricks – daring feats of dexterity that pushed the limits of his ability. But would the cocky executive or the powerful CEO have realized that one trick is physically harder than another? After all, if you do things right, your audience shouldn't be aware of any difficulty in the first place. So, rather than striving towards an arbitrary technical goal, Richard used those restaurant years as an experimental laboratory for learning to manage an audience.

Richard also talks about the importance of silence. 'A lot of magicians think that if the audience are not clapping or laughing, they're not enjoying it,' he told me. 'But that's not necessarily the case at all. That's a harsh lesson. Silence does feel awkward, but actually people are thinking, they're evaluating, they're processing. Silence is massively useful, providing it's done with warmth and sensitivity.' Every trick, he said, needs time to land. Lots of magicians are in a hurry to do the next one. But that's a mistake.

As a doctor, becoming comfortable with silence is equally important – and equally difficult to learn. That's what I was doing with Sarah in my consulting room, as I waited for her to process our conversation. Silence is not just the absence of speech; it provides space for a different kind of communication. As the GP and psychotherapist John Launer put it to me once, 'Two silences can also be a conversation.' But we tend to leap in and talk instead of listening. We shy away from silence and we rush to fill the space.

When we listen instead of talking, our attention is where it should be – on those our work is for. Listening, then, is a hallmark of being expert. We cannot be in broadcast mode all the time. When we are doing something for others, we need to be quiet and pay attention. The communicative aspects of our work, the ebb and flow between performer and audience, require transmission, reception and silence.

The best advice Richard's magic teacher gave him was to go and see other magicians perform – but to watch the spectators, not the performer. Standing towards the back of a crowd, Richard learned to recognize the tiny signals of an audience's involvement. He registered those telltale flickers of an eye that show when someone is not completely absorbed. He taught himself to read each audience's collective response. Then he applied this to his own performance. He became like a shepherd corralling sheep, guiding them towards their pen and recognizing when they were moving as one. He came to understand how to steer them to where he wanted them to go, mentally as well as physically.

Magicians have a dictum about audiences: 'If you want them to look at something, look at *it*; if you want them to look at you, look at *them*.' It never fails. If you look at someone, they can't help looking at you; it's hardwired into us as humans. And this apparently simple insight turns out to be remarkably powerful. When you can shape and direct someone's attention, you can apply that skill to all kinds of settings, from social gatherings to a professional performance.

But the dictum has a corollary. If you *don't* want them to look at something, don't look at it. Anyone who has consulted a doctor, a financial adviser, or been for a job interview knows what it's like when someone fixes their eyes on a computer screen instead of engaging with you. You are drawn to what they are looking at, whether you can see it or not. The invisible thread between you and them has been broken.

Showing that your attention is on something other than the person you are with sends powerful signals that you are not interested. Yet, as a professional, it's easy to focus on the requirements of your job, such as entering data into a computer system or looking something up online, rather than thinking of the experience of the person you're with.

As you become expert, the component skills of your

craft must become instinctive. Returning to the theories we examined in Chapter 3, you'll remember that we move from a cognitive through an associative to an autonomous stage of becoming expert, eventually gaining enough experience for the 'doing' to look after itself. At the Royal College of Music, they say that when you go out on stage as a student, you must have practised so much that your best performance is good enough. But when you go out there as a professional, your *worst* performance must be good enough. That involves going far beyond the point at which you think you have perfected what you're going to play. You must be able to rely on your skills whatever happens, even if you're terrified or insecure, or things go unexpectedly wrong.

The textbooks refer to this as 'over-learning'. You have to be able to perform under all circumstances, but especially when you have additional challenges. You must be able to carve, cut or sew not only when your materials and tools are compliant and of high quality, but also when there are flaws in the stone or wood, or your instruments are blunt or missing. You must be able to perform when your body is below par; when you're tired, unwell, stressed or anxious. You have to know what it feels like to be at or beyond the edge of what you are used to – or what you, your materials and the situation will tolerate without falling apart. You have to satisfy the audience, regardless of how you are feeling.

A performance to remember

You also have to shape how people will remember an encounter, whether a magic show or a consultation with a doctor. Will Houstoun, another magician I've worked with, says that every magic trick takes place three times. The first is when the magician does it. The second is when an audience member thinks about it afterwards, replaying it in their mind and trying to work out what happened. The third time is when they tell someone else about it. Each time, the story changes slightly. Expert magicians are adept at shaping things so their audience remembers what the performer wants, rather than what actually happened.

It's not only magicians who do this. Experts design the conditions for selective recollection, focusing attention on some areas and directing it away from others. Though people don't go to the doctor to be entertained, they should still leave with a positive impression of the encounter, even though studies show that patients retain little of what was actually said. What they do remember is how the consultation made them feel. When someone leaves, they need to do so with the sense that the consultation has helped, and to feel that the doctor has attended to their experience and cared for them. They need to feel that the consultation hasn't been about the doctor, but about them.

This isn't only true for doctors and magicians, of

course. It holds true for every realm of expert practice where there is a performance component. It's remembering how having a builder in our house made us feel, long after the job itself is finished. It's why people return to Fabrice the hairstylist – it's not simply that they liked the style he gave them; they remember enjoying having him cut their hair.

Learning to listen

Back in my consulting room with Sarah, I have to decide what to do next. I know what she needs medically – blood tests, CT scans and an urgent referral to a specialist. But all this is going to be difficult for her to take in. I don't want to mislead her. I can't tell her everything is going to be fine when I'm pretty sure it won't be; I have to be honest. If I'm right and she has got cancer, we'll be seeing a lot of one another in the months to come. We'll need to trust one another. My role will be to curate her experience of being ill, to shape it and ensure it's as good as it can be. To do that, I have to go at her pace, not force her to fit in with mine. I need to give her time, make space, keep quiet and listen. So how do I take things forward?

At first I don't say anything, but instead just sit quietly and wait. Then she says, 'I've been wondering if it might be something more serious this time. Could it . . . ?'

After a few moments, I say, 'Maybe we've both been

thinking along the same lines. I could be wrong, and I hope I am, but I'm concerned by what you've told me and we need to find out more. I'd like to arrange some tests, then an appointment at the hospital with a specialist. How would you feel about that?'

Sarah gives a reluctant sigh. 'All right, Doctor,' she says. 'Let's do that.' We both know that this is just the beginning of the story, but at least I'm not steamrollering Sarah with something she's not ready to hear.

As we talk, Sarah confides that she's thought for a while that something might be seriously wrong. She hasn't wanted to admit it, because of everything else going on in her life. She doesn't have time to be ill. She feels she can't cope with what a serious diagnosis might entail, because too many people depend on her. By the end of our consultation, she lets me arrange some tests and refer her to a specialist.

It turns out that she does have cancer, as we had both half suspected. From then on, the medical pathway seems mapped out – surgery, post-operative recovery, convalescence. But Sarah has a cancer of the pancreas, which is why the whites of her eyes have gone yellow from jaundice. Pancreatic malignancy is a particularly horrible form of cancer, and my heart sinks when the diagnosis is confirmed.

Over the weeks and months that follow, Sarah and I do see a lot of one another. What frightens Sarah most isn't the pain, or even dying. It's being taken into hospital and being alone. She fears for her family if she's gone. So that's what we spend most of our time talking about. It isn't my medical knowledge she needs most, but time to talk.

Later on, I recognize I was helping Sarah through an experience, not treating a disease. The best care I could give her was not in telling her about the science behind the drugs that would slow the cancer, or the operations she would undergo, or the technicalities of the test results and data. All of that played a role, and I needed to understand it so I could help guide her decisions. But my real job was to free up my attention and listen. The best medicine I could offer was to shift my focus to her.

So let's review the principles I've been describing. First, you become confident in the physical aspects of your work – cutting a fringe, doing magic tricks, making a jacket or a diagnosis. You practise, practise, practise until it becomes second nature. In time, you become so proficient that you can do it even when your materials are unruly, you're feeling below par or you're working in challenging conditions.

Then you throw your attention outwards, focusing on the people your work is for. You develop an awareness of how they respond, using the attentional capacity you have released by all that practice to notice and interpret the non-verbal cues of whoever you are with. Finally, you think about the impression you want them to take away when they leave. Your aim is to bring the encounter to a graceful close, with something you are proud to have achieved and the other person is glad to have experienced.

This chapter has explored that transition from gaining individual knowledge and skill to using that skill for the benefit of others. An initial 'selfish' phase of becoming expert must give way to 'sharing'. But until your skills have become second nature, you can't move beyond them to focus on your performance as a whole. If you can't make a coin vanish every time, you can't engage your audience. If you're not sure *how* to operate, you can't decide *when* to operate. If you feel insecure with fast passages when you're playing music in a group, you're not listening to the players around you or thinking about your audience. If you're trying to remember the seventeen causes of breathlessness, you're not able to hear what your patient is – and more importantly *isn't* – telling you. You may miss those tiny signals that give a clue to what is really going on.

Though this transition from you to them is easy to miss out, it's a crucial step as you start to develop your unique style. But shifting your focus from yourself to other people doesn't mean your own personality disappears. Quite the opposite, in fact. It's your personality that makes you the unique expert you're becoming. That's what we'll explore in the next chapter.

8. Developing voice

My consulting room door opens and Harry comes in. It's a busy morning at my Wiltshire practice; I've got a stack of patients waiting and I'm feeling under pressure. I've met Harry a couple of times, but I don't know him well. He's in his early seventies, with nicotine-stained fingers and a bit of a wheeze. As soon as Harry sits down, I ask him what the problem is. He tells me he's had a cough for several weeks, and he seems worried that there might be something more to it. He doesn't look well, and I feel a bit uneasy. I take out his notes, flicking through his medical history. I'm about to ask him some questions when the consultation freezes. My tutor has paused the tape.

I'm spending a week at a residential college for adult education. I'm on a course to become a GP trainer. If I'm successful, we'll be able to have trainees attached to our practice – doctors who have decided to become GPs themselves. They'll have spent several years working in a hospital as junior doctors, usually on six-month rotations like I did. They'll probably have worked in paediatrics, general medicine and perhaps psychiatry. Then they'll spend a year in a practice, learning on the job under the supervision of their GP trainer. There, they'll learn how different general practice can be from hospital medicine, and they'll spend a lot of time studying and practising the skills of consultation. Every week they'll have an afternoon with their trainer, discussing cases and honing their skills. At first, like me when I started, they'll probably feel rudderless and disoriented, swamped by patients with apparently trivial conditions but terrified of missing one with a serious disease. It will take them a while to understand what general practice is really about. That's where I'll come in as a trainer.

Supervising a trainee, like treating patients, requires a lot of skill. It starts with having insight into your own practice as a doctor. That's what we're learning on the course, and that's why we're starting by analysing our own consultations before helping our trainees with theirs. For most of that week I'm in a room with our tutor Clive, as well as five other doctors who are learning to become trainers. Clive's been a GP for decades, and he's got years of experience in training trainers. He doesn't say much, but his silences are more eloquent than words.

We're watching videos we've recorded over the last couple of weeks. Clive asked us to bring examples of ordinary consultations, not ones we're especially pleased with. But, of course, we've all chosen ones we're proud of. Nobody has brought anything disastrous, and we've each tried to slip in some that show how clever we've been. Like me, the other GPs think we'll be analysing these encounters and looking for diagnostic brilliance, medical knowledge, technical skill. But we don't. Instead, Clive is making us look at *how* we consult.

I've been in general practice for several years at this point, and I've become reasonably comfortable with consultations. But it has always been just me and my patient. There's been nobody else watching, let alone a group of my peers.

Now it's my turn to be in the spotlight, and I'm terrified. I feel my reputation is on the line. I'm waiting for Clive's comments about the likely cause of Harry's cough. Instead he looks at me thoughtfully and says, 'I wonder how you're making Harry *feel* . . .' Then he sits quietly and waits.

Developing your voice

When Clive asked how I thought I was making Harry feel, he wasn't talking about the cause of his cough. He was talking about Harry's experience of being with me in my consulting room. From this perspective, a clinical consultation is an encounter between a professional performer (in this case, me) and an audience (in this case, Harry). The audience's experience of the performance is shaped by the performer's 'voice'. That's what makes each doctor's style unique. In the previous chapter we looked at how you put yourself aside, focusing instead on your patient, your client or whoever your work is for.

Now we'll look at how you bring yourself back in – how you develop voice.

Paul Haidet, a jazz musician and family doctor at Penn State College of Medicine in the United States, has studied this in detail. He writes about an expert's ability to 'drop' what they have learned formally but still draw on it in the moment as they respond to what is happening around them. He sees parallels between medicine and music, too. As a jazz musician, you spend years with your instrument, practising scales, learning repertoire, mastering theory, developing techniques. But then the ones who make a mark, as Haidet puts it, are those 'who channel the theory, technique and ideas of their predecessors through their own personalities, feelings and experiences'. This is what jazz musicians call 'developing voice'. That's how you instantly recognize a recording of Miles Davis, Chet Baker or Freddie Hubbard from the first couple of notes, if you know that kind of music.

Jeremy Jackman, former counter-tenor in the King's Singers vocal ensemble, explained voice to me like this: 'When you're a small child and your mother reads you a bedtime story, you get used to how she reads it. When your Aunt Ethel comes to stay and she reads you that story, the words are the same but the story sounds different. Her voice – not just literally, but how she interprets the words and the meaning – is unique. It's like that with music too.'

Something similar happens in all fields. My wife makes hats, and I can spot one of her hats in a room full of other people's. Similarly, if you gave me a page of writing by John le Carré, one of my favourite writers, I'd be able to know it was him rather than John D. Mac-Donald, whose crime novels I also devour. In your own work, whatever that may be, your voice is what differentiates you from your colleagues.

Voice dictates how you implement the 'it's not about you' of the previous chapter. This is especially relevant in performances where your audience is very small. In medicine, that audience is often just one person. Even with a family consultation, it's seldom more than three or four.

Voice is how you tell one doctor from another. I had to learn how to recognize and acknowledge my voice as a doctor, and how to use that for my patients. In this chapter, we'll explore what happens when we think of experts as close-up live performers with a very small audience. We'll look at *how* to perform, and how developing your voice is part of becoming expert.

As doctors on that course for aspiring GP trainers, we'd passed the point where we were talking about medical knowledge. Anyone becoming a GP will already have spent years in the initial stages of becoming expert. They'll have done time and learned to touch, feel and see. They'll have made a lot of mistakes and put them right. They'll have grappled with the need to keep all that knowledge and skill out of view, to make the 'it's not about you' transition we examined in Chapter 7. But they may not have thought about voice. Yet voice is essential to performance. It captures your uniqueness, your style. Developing voice is something we all do as we internalize and transform what we've learned, and use it to become ourselves – whether as a plumber, an accountant or anything else.

There's no such thing as a perfect suit

Joshua the tailor has voice too. He likes working with all kinds of customers, not just the straightforward ones; for Joshua, this is a challenge to relish. Unlike many of his contemporaries, he deliberately sought out difficult or unusual clients while he was training. Sometimes the challenges were physical – people with asymmetries, spinal deformities or differently shaped limbs. At other times the challenges were about personality – people who were aggressive or demanding, obsessed by detail or difficult to please. The other tailors were delighted when he took those customers, as it gave them an easier life.

Joshua's second apprenticeship was with Arthur, a master cutting tailor. It was Arthur who taught him the principles of designing a suit from scratch. That allowed Joshua to create something unique for each client, something that suited that man's personality and met his needs. After Arthur retired, Joshua left that tailoring house and set up his own business in partnership with his wife. That's when he established his voice as an independent craftsman. No longer constrained by bosses and colleagues, by 'how we do things around here', he was free to bring together the skills he had learned and establish his own identity.

Early on in becoming a tailor, Joshua realized that there were many possible solutions to any problem. 'There is no perfect suit,' he explained to me. 'You are always striking a balance, a compromise between what the suit looks like on the hanger and what it feels like on the man. A garment is always an interpretation. You have to recognize and respond to people's instinctive reactions, whether they are aware of those reactions or not. Otherwise they won't be truly happy with what you create.'

Part of the satisfaction for Joshua was the clothes he designed, the end product of his work. But what excited him most was the opportunity to work with people and find out what they wanted. This is more difficult than it sounds.

With the freedom of developing your voice comes responsibility. As you stop being a cipher in someone else's workshop and develop your individuality as an expert, you accept responsibility for what you do. Once Joshua started his own business and could become the kind of tailor he wanted to be, he had to make it work. He had to live with the consequences of his decisions. During his years of doing time, learning to see and to do, he had absorbed and internalized the style of his masters. His work at that time was recognizably that of the tailoring house he was employed by, and he had the security of working in an organization. Now he was on his own, creating his own style and curating each client's experience of having a suit or jacket made by him. He was developing his voice.

By the time I started thinking of my voice as a GP, I was an experienced doctor. It was over twenty years since I'd started as a medical student, spending all those hours in a formalin-filled fug in the dissecting room and doing the bloods on a hospital ward. It was easy to forget how I'd struggled in those early days of doing time, learning to see and to touch, and the other steps I've described in this book. But, outside medicine, I was still going through those initial stages. And they came flooding back when I started to play my harpsichord.

Music and other people

Though I'd finished assembling my instrument from the kit, I barely knew how to play it. To begin with, I practised on my own and tried to get the hang of it. I'd learned the piano as a child and had taken up the pipe organ as a junior doctor, but I'd never played with other people. While the harpsichord has a huge solo repertoire, much of its music is performed in a group. It seemed a shame to keep my instrument to myself, though I was nervous about playing with others. So I took a deep breath, then signed up for a weekend residential course on baroque chamber music. I managed to squeeze my harpsichord into the car and I set off.

There were about thirty of us, all amateurs. Some, like me, were just beginning. Others were more experienced, and some were technically pretty advanced. Helping us to make sense of it all were three expert tutors. In the first session I found myself in a group with a cellist, a violinist and a recorder player. Our tutor gave us a pile of sheet music by composers I'd never heard of, and told us to get on with it. Sonatas, suites, dances – the pop music of its day. We didn't practise, we just played each one through at sight, then went on to the next. A lot of the pieces were repetitive and rather boring, but we played them anyway.

As a harpsichordist, I was in the continuo section. This is in the background most of the time, like the rhythm section in a jazz band. The cello plays the bass line as written by the composer, and the harpsichord fills in with harmonies. Continuo performers in the baroque period would have been expert at doing this, but I'd never played with others before, let alone tried to sight-read an unfamiliar piece.

Continuo playing gives a lot of freedom, as you're not expected to play only what's on the page. But there's also a lot of responsibility, because you have to fill out the bass line with chords, supporting but not competing with the others in the group. You play from a 'figured bass' – numerical codes that tell you the harmonies the composer intended. It's like trying to do a crossword puzzle while reading aloud and cooking a soufflé at the same time. I wondered how I would cope. I was terrified of getting lost or playing a wrong note.

The first thing I learned was that nobody really cared what I played. They were all concentrating on their own parts, and they only became aware of me if I got in the way or made a blunder. I was like the mantelpiece clock that you only notice when it stops ticking. From being the centre of my own attention, I became someone who made a small twangly noise in the background. As one of the tutors put it: 'Just keep going, Roger. Even if every note you play is wrong. As long as you start together and finish together, what happens in between isn't so important.'

Playing in that group made me listen – really listen – to the musicians around me. Instead of focusing on my hands, or on my skill (or lack of it) as a harpsichordist, I had to think how I would contribute. At first, I was scared that I'd lose my place and make an idiot of myself. Then I realized that sitting right next to me was an excellent cellist, and that we were playing the same bass line. If I felt overwhelmed, I knew that she would keep going, allowing me to skip a few bars and get back on the rails by listening to her. All I had to do was find my place, play the single bass line on the written page, and make sure I was in tempo with the other players. Then I could start to think about how to fill in the harmonies. To do that, I had to widen my attentional focus, to be aware of the ensemble as a whole and to listen.

At first I was happy to blend in without being noticed. But over time, something surprising happened. I became aware that I wasn't an interchangeable cipher; I was making an essential contribution after all. I realized that *how* I played was as important as *what* I played. I found I was developing a style, a way of playing that was recognizably mine. It wasn't just whether I played the right notes, but how I became part of the ensemble. I learned that less is more, that people valued the way I remained inconspicuous, didn't put in needless flourishes, avoided showing off. And the way I did that was distinctive. This was my voice.

I went to these workshops for several years running. One year, there were three of us harpsichord players. When we were deciding who would play with whom, a cellist I remembered from a previous course told me she'd like me to be in her group. 'You're the one who listens,' she said. I felt very proud. I'd developed my own approach to continuo playing; I was starting to create my own style. Of course, I wasn't expert – far from it. Playing the harpsichord is a hobby for me, not a career. But I had made a transition that was immensely satisfying, and it made all those hours of practice worthwhile. I was able to play in my own way and be part of making music I'd always loved to listen to. My identity as a harpsichordist had moved up a level.

The immensity of the problem

Voice isn't only about what you say and how you say it. It involves all of the senses. It includes how you engage with people, how you relate to them, how you touch them and how you respond when they touch you. Voice shapes how you navigate the space between you and whoever you are with. It can also be expressed by how you configure the physical setting you work in. My GP partners and I put a lot of thought into how we designed the consulting rooms in our practice. We wanted our patients to feel comfortable and able to talk, but we also needed to be able to carry out clinical examinations. Each GP made different concessions, and their choices reflected their personality.

Staring at my own consulting room on the frozen video screen at the GP trainers course, Clive, the other doctors and I considered how it reflected my approach. Then we restarted my consultation with Harry about his cough. We watched another thirty seconds. On the screen, I was starting to listen to Harry's chest with my stethoscope. Clive suddenly paused the tape again and said, 'Why are you doing that?'

I was nonplussed. Surely it was obvious. Listening with a stethoscope is part of making a diagnosis; it's what doctors do. The mantra of 'inspection, palpation, percussion, auscultation' is so deeply embedded from my medical-school days that I'd never thought to question it. But Clive wanted to know what was going through my mind when I picked up my stethoscope – what I was planning to do next.

One of the other GPs said, 'I use my stethoscope to buy time while I think what I'm going to say.' Another told us, 'I use mine to reassure my patients that I know what I'm doing, that I've got knowledge and skill, so they trust me when I give them a diagnosis.' I hadn't thought of it like that before, but it made a lot of sense. Sometimes a stethoscope is just a stethoscope, but often it's more. A stethoscope is a symbol of our profession, and people expect you to use it.

Clive pointed out that we would all have managed this consultation differently and that we'd probably all be equally effective, despite our differences in approach. At medical school I'd been taught that each patient had a diagnosis and that our task was to find it. But for Clive, it wasn't as simple as that. He made me focus on my individual way of being a doctor, on my performance and my voice.

Developing voice is part of the Journeyman phase. It's when you shift from being able to do some of the things experts do to starting to become expert yourself. It's when you develop your own ways of responding to whoever you are with and dealing with the unexpected. But this needs a combination of humility and self-confidence, and that's a difficult balance to achieve.

As you develop voice, you're not abandoning what you have learned; you're reshaping it. As we saw with the music groups I took part in, you don't have to wait years for this to happen. The steps we've explored don't happen in strict linear order, and they often overlap. For instance, if you've already become expert in one area then it can help when you move into another, as Joshua found with his second apprenticeship. But all the time you're moving towards independence, towards becoming comfortable with your own way of doing things. You're creating an identity.

As you develop your voice, you realize that technical skill is necessary but not sufficient. It's how you apply that skill that matters. You must know a lot and be able to do a lot, but only bring out what's relevant in that moment. You must avoid showing off. Performers have known this for centuries. Staying with baroque music for a moment longer, C. P. E. Bach (one of Johann Sebastian Bach's many sons) wrote *An Essay on the True Art of Playing Keyboard Instruments*, published in 1753. Discussing technique and interpretation, he said: 'Keyboardists whose chief asset is mere technique are clearly at a disadvantage . . . They overwhelm our hearing without satisfying it and stun the mind without moving it . . . A mere technician, however, can lay no claim to the rewards of those who sway in gentle undulation the ear rather than the eye, the heart rather than the ear, and lead it where they will.' The ability to sway the ear in gentle undulation is what an expert does.

Over two hundred years later, in 1966, the legendary jazz pianist Bill Evans recorded a conversation with his brother Harry in which they talked about Bill's approach to playing. He'd developed this a decade earlier, shutting himself up in his garage in 1954 for over a year to work on his technique. He went right back to basics, even though he'd already been playing professionally. In that conversation, Bill says:

> The whole process of learning to play jazz is to take these problems from the outer level in, one by one, and to stay with it at a very intense, conscious-concentration level until that process becomes secondary and subconscious ... Most people just don't realize the immensity of the problem and, either because they can't conquer it immediately, think that they haven't got the ability, or they're so impatient to conquer it that they never do see it through ... They would rather approximate the entire problem than to take a small part of it and be real and true about it. To approximate the whole thing in a vague way gives you a feeling that you've more or less touched the thing, but in this way you just lead yourself toward confusion and ultimately you're going to get so confused that you'll never find your way out ... If you try to approximate something that is very advanced and don't know what you're doing, you can't advance.

Evans puts his finger on something important here. As we develop our individuality, we watch and copy experts we admire. But until we have been through what they have been through, there's no point trying to copy their flourishes. Developing your voice emerges from the initial stages of hard graft and rigour, and you can't short-circuit the process. You can imitate experts, but you can't yet do what they are really doing. Like Bill Evans in his garage, you have to work that out for yourself.

Those senior consultants who listened quietly on a ward round when I was a young doctor, then came up with a new diagnosis, could only do that because of their years of experience. Those GPs who just seemed to 'know' what questions to ask had gone through a similar process. As a trainee, I could imitate their behaviour as much as I liked, but I had nothing to base my pronouncements on. Your voice has to reflect an inner state of being expert, or you'll only be able to use it in circumstances you have already encountered. You'll struggle at the margins when things start to unravel. To be expert, your voice must remain recognizably yours, even when you are in situations you haven't encountered before.

That ability starts with the steps outlined in Chapters 1 to 5. You have to have spent months and years acquiring the skills of your craft or profession, getting them under your belt and making them second nature. You have to know that you can work to a consistent standard, and that you have mastered your core skills. You have to know you can give a good performance in any circumstances – even when you are feeling tired, out of sorts, or working with unruly materials under challenging conditions.

Voice is tied up with identity and confidence, with

who and what you believe yourself to be. It wasn't until well after I qualified that I felt I had really 'become' a doctor. Before that, I knew a lot of the things that doctors knew, and I could do a lot of the things that doctors did, but I hadn't become one myself. Gradually I became comfortable with my new identity – for a while, at least.

Then I started my surgical training and the same thing happened again. For years I would say 'I'm training to become a surgeon', even when I was leading surgical teams in big, difficult operations. I hadn't yet settled into *being* a surgeon. Eventually that changed, and by the time I became a consultant ten years later, if someone asked me what I did I'd say, 'I'm a surgeon.' The process repeated itself when I became a GP, and again when I became an academic. Voice isn't as straightforward as it sounds.

To be effective, voice must be authentic. You are drawing on aspects of yourself that are already there, not creating a new identity. You adapt and respond to each situation and the people that you're with. For instance, similar to my harpsichord playing style, I wanted to be a doctor who listened and responded to each patient's tempo. First I would fit in, and then start to shape the conversation. I might speed things up or slow them down. I would conduct the consultation while allowing my patient the freedom to express what they wanted. I would try to keep the whole context in mind, balancing the needs of the patient I was with and those of the others waiting outside.

The subtle seductions of voice

At this stage in the path of becoming expert, you are learning to hold two aspects in creative tension: bedrock knowledge and performance in the moment. In the early stages, the emphasis is on knowledge, skills and joining a community of practice. As you start to fly solo, taking more responsibility for your own actions, your style and personality become more prominent. As we've seen, that's when your voice emerges. But there are pitfalls if your voice becomes too idiosyncratic and you lose touch with how it lands.

A patient going through the menopause told me she'd seen a female doctor about her symptoms. 'Think of it like this,' the doctor had told her. 'Your body is changing. You used to be a plum. Now you're becoming a prune.' I know what the doctor meant, but many people would have been offended by her choice of words. Fortunately, this patient found it hilarious. But voice is a double-edged sword. Because you are using your own personality as a tool, you need self-awareness and sensitivity to monitor how you come across to other people. You have to recognize that your way of putting things may not have the effect you intended.

When I was a medical student in Manchester, I spent time in an infertility clinic with a consultant gynaecologist. He'd start each consultation by explaining some basic medical facts. 'Humans reproduce by eggs, like chickens,' he would say, 'only human eggs are much smaller and they're inside. Do you understand?' On one occasion, the patient listened attentively without saying anything. For some reason, the consultant paused and asked her if she had a job. 'Yes – I'm a lecturer, here at the university,' she replied. 'What do you lecture on?' he asked. 'Human reproductive biology,' she said. The consultant had the grace to look abashed for a moment, but then, alarmingly, he carried on with his spiel exactly as he had done a thousand times before.

Whether it's gynaecology or graphic design, it's no use having a 'standard' approach. Salespeople know they can't use the same patter every time they pitch. That quickly becomes inauthentic, and prevents either party really listening. Your voice is not just *what* you say, or even how you say it. It's the means by which you engage – whether with a patient, client, colleague or customer. It's how you connect.

Experts' handling of voice can be impressive – a lot goes on under the surface. The most skilful GPs I ever met seemed able to put their finger on a patient's problem with no apparent effort. They weren't displaying medical knowledge, they were just listening – and maybe doing a little talking. They didn't drive things, or insist on asking questions in a specified order. They didn't show off. They seemed able to crystallize any problem without effort. Yet ask them afterwards what was going on and their language would switch in a flash. They would describe how they'd been considering this diagnosis or that, and weighing up the chances that it might be something serious. They'd talk about recent papers they had read, or how they were thinking about referring the patient to one specialist or another. They would have made contingency plans and put safety nets in place in case they'd got things wrong. Yet none of this was obvious. For their patients, the consultation was just something natural: a conversation that helped.

Joshua does something similar when he's with a client. He's quietly confident and competent, making sensible suggestions and helping each person navigate the many choices confronting them. But scratch the surface and you find his knowledge is encyclopedic. He's not only an expert in the design and construction of suits, he also knows about style and the history of fashion and materials. You wouldn't necessarily be aware of that, because he only brings it out when he needs it.

But voice can have a dark side too. Voice is so powerful that it can hide laziness or lack of knowledge. Its very power makes it open to corruption or abuse. Bravura performance can conceal ignorance, or mask unjustified self-confidence. If deficiencies in knowledge and skill are overcompensated for by dazzling performance, voice can morph into charisma or mere charm. Factual knowledge can fray, and skills degrade. I saw this with senior clinicians whose medical knowledge was drifting out of date but whose performance continued to improve.

Their facility at a personal level concealed a disconnection from advances in the wider world. Most of the time little harm resulted, but the asymmetry in power between an apparent expert (the doctor) and an apparent non-expert (the patient) meant that such people often went unchallenged. Sometimes their lack of up-to-date knowledge led to disaster, and an important diagnosis was missed.

So, there is a fine line to tread. Too far in one direction and you are a mechanical dispenser of textbook information, purveying formulaic, preformed solutions which may not address the real problem. Too far in the other direction and it's all about you again, a self-indulgent focus on your personality and performance. Experts steer a path between these twin dangers – between suppressing their voice and relying on it too much. They avoid placing too much emphasis on personality and too little on knowledge and skill.

Neither the first nor the last

One of the benefits of age and experience is the wisdom which allows experts to cast a sceptical eye over the latest trends and fashions. This avoids being swept up in a froth of enthusiasm, and ensures that decisions are tempered by common sense. It makes me think of Alexander Pope's adage in his *Essay on Criticism*, which was often quoted to me when I was a medical student.

In words as fashions the same rule will hold;
Alike fantastic, if too new, or old:
Be not the first by whom the new are tried,
Nor yet the last to lay the old aside.

Yet it can be difficult to distinguish this balanced, healthy scepticism from being too lazy to learn new techniques or keep abreast of new technologies. It's often said that our world privileges information over knowledge, and knowledge over wisdom. The ability to stay calm, take the long view and be thoughtful about embracing new technologies is increasingly rare and valuable. Level-headed guidance about what to believe is important now more than ever. For that, we need the wisdom of experts – in medicine and everywhere else.

We trust people, not faceless dispensers of facts. It's through someone's voice – their style, their individuality, their capacity to relate to us as individuals – that we decide whether or not to give them that trust. One doctor, one hairstylist, one tailor, is not the same as another.

Experts have a responsibility not to abuse our trust, nor hide behind it to conceal slothfulness, malign intent or self-interest. All these things happen. Close-up magicians can become cheats and card sharps; well-known artists can pass off pieces of shoddy quality because their work is sought after; surgeons can do unnecessary operations to supplement their income. Such a misplacing of true purpose is a corruption of the responsibility of care, as we saw earlier with the surgeons who liked to 'cut'.

This is the dark side of the switch from you to them – a distortion which moves the focus back from them to you. It's an abuse of the power of voice.

Back to Harry and his cough. A few weeks after my time at the GP trainers course, he comes to see me in my surgery; then again a short time after that. I've been thinking a lot about him in the meantime. Something is obviously bothering him, but I can't work out what. I try to think what might lie behind his repeated visits. The next time he comes I try a different tack. On an earlier occasion he mentioned Ethel, his wife, but didn't say much about her. I have a feeling there might be more. 'You know when we were talking the other day and you told me about Ethel . . . ?' I begin.

I stop talking and wait. In a few moments, it all comes pouring out. It turns out that it isn't Harry's cough that's been worrying him most. It is Ethel, who is bed-bound at home. He's terrified that if something serious happened to him, she'd be stranded and there'd be no one to take care of her. So although in a way he does want to know what's wrong with him, in another way he doesn't. From then on, our conversations are different and we're able to think of possible solutions. In the end, Harry agrees to have an X-ray and some other tests. It turns out he has emphysema but fortunately no cancer. Still, we spend most of our time talking about Ethel, and I think these conversations help him as much as treating his cough.

Going back to those weekends of baroque music, I realized that I didn't have to be a virtuoso to express my voice at the harpsichord. Just as well, as I never will be. In that setting, it was more important to blend in with others, to contribute without seeking the limelight and – to paraphrase Bill Evans – to know that the problem is large, that I have to take it a step at a time and to enjoy this step-by-step learning procedure.

If you've reached this point in your path to becoming expert, you have arrived at a watershed. For a great many people, like me with my harpsichord, this is enough. I'm able to play to a standard that pleases me. If you want to go further, you can take the next step. But moving from here to becoming truly expert may well be the greatest leap of all.

9. Learning to improvise

Back to South Africa in the 1980s and another emergency in the operating theatre. This time my patient is Themba, a young man with a small stab wound in the side of his neck near the angle of his jaw. He's anaesthetized on the operating table and I'm about to begin. It's a busy Saturday intake and several theatres are running at once. The other surgeons are on call, operating on their own patients. I've been at Bara for over two years now and I've reached the stage where I should be able to do an operation like this on my own. But, as I discovered when I was operating on Jonas (see Chapter 6), the neck can be treacherous territory.

We clean and drape Themba, then I make an incision along the line of his sternomastoid, the muscle that runs from behind the ear to the breastbone. I'm excited and terrified. At the best of times, a stabbed neck is a challenge. You never know what you'll find – the size of the wound and the extent of the damage can be wildly out of proportion. Mentally, I go over what I might encounter: the strap muscles, nerves and blood vessels.

As soon as I start the operation I realize I'm in for a nasty shock. None of the structures I'd learned about from books and in the dissecting room seem to be there.

No tidy strap muscles, no arteries and certainly no nerves. Those little buggers in the neck I spent so long memorizing have disappeared. It's all just a horrible squidgy mess, and everything I touch oozes blood. The knife must have punctured a major artery which is now pumping blood into the tissues of the neck and obliterating familiar landmarks.

What if I can't handle the situation, if I can't find the injury? What if other crucial structures have been divided? What if I damage something vital during the operation? What if Themba bleeds to death on the operating table? I've never encountered a situation like this before, so I'll have to improvise. But how?

The art of improvisation

At this point, you've reached the next cusp on the trajectory of becoming expert. You've done time, used your senses and have a fully operational mise en place. You're a seasoned professional, a Journeyman who recognizes that 'it's not about you', and you've developed your own style or voice.

In this chapter, we'll explore how you develop the higher-order skills of responding to the complex demands of a rapidly evolving situation – in a word, *improvising*. Part of this is how you come up with solutions that get you out of trouble. But being able to improvise is more than that. Improvising is what experts do – it's what makes experts expert. And that's across the board: in every field of activity, experts have to improvise.

Years after that operation on Themba, I was in the audience during a gig at the London Jazz Festival when something went wrong. I was listening to a trio – piano, bass and tenor sax – and they were playing new material written by the pianist. They had handwritten sheets on their music stands. The pianist was facing away from the audience, the bass player was at the back of the stage and the saxophonist at the front. Halfway through the first set, I became aware of a brief hiccup in the rhythm, a sense of something unexpected. Almost immediately, everything settled down, and I wouldn't have given it a second thought if the bass player hadn't spoken up after the number to explain what had happened.

Although he and the pianist had played together before, he told us, they had never worked with this saxophonist and they hadn't had a chance to rehearse. Halfway through the number, the bass player noticed that his written part had some extra bars and he was getting out of sync with the others. Realizing that there must be a transcription error, he had to act fast. So he'd looked over to the sax player's music stand, transposed what he saw into the bass clef and continued playing. A combination of swift thinking and sangfroid, rooted in decades of experience.

Though the stakes were very different, the bass player's description took me back to that scary night in Soweto when I was operating on Themba's stabbed neck. It made me think that a jazz band is like a surgical team, encountering the unexpected and responding as a group. Then I started to think not in terms of surgery or music, but of improvisation as a characteristic of being expert, something that could apply to any field. I began to wonder whether insights from other experts might shed light on the excitement and terror of dealing with the unexpected.

When you're talking about jazz and you use the word 'improvisation', people usually think about the music. They might imagine a trumpet player stepping to the front of the stage, picking up a musical theme and taking it in new directions, responding in the moment to ideas that seem to come from nowhere. They think of improvisation as something spontaneous, effortless and requiring very little preparation. Most of the time that couldn't be further from the truth. That may be what it looks like, but it's not what's going on beneath the surface.

Improvisation is based on years of hard graft. It builds on all the steps I've explored in the book so far. It starts with doing time, using your senses and working within a system. In addition to practising, learning to listen, getting things wrong and putting them right, improvisers have to have made the transition 'from you to them'. For a musician, the 'them' is the other musicians they're playing with and the audience they're playing for. At the same time they've developed their voice, the unique style that makes them the experts they are becoming.

But improvising isn't an occasional departure from being able to do things properly. Improvising *is* being able to do things properly. Being able to improvise effectively is a high point of becoming an expert.

When I was watching that jazz band, there was already plenty of improvisation going on in their performance. Improvisation is an inherent part of jazz music – not all of the music is written out; the musicians have to come up with something on the spot. This is where all those hours of practice and theory come in. Knowing which notes in a melody will work with the underlying harmony – and stringing them together into something expressive or moving – can only happen when the production of each note is second nature. The ability to play jazz music, I would say, is having expertise. But what I saw on that day was something even more impressive. When it became clear that the expectations underpinning the improvisation had been broken, the bassist was able to come up with a solution in the moment in a way that his colleagues understood and most of the audience weren't aware of. That, I would say, is being expert.

Some improvisation takes your breath away. On 24 January 1975, the American jazz musician Keith Jarrett played a concert at the Cologne Opera House. It's now seen as a tour de force of improvisation, and has gone down in history as a landmark performance. But the Köln Concert (as it's usually known) almost didn't happen. Jarrett was in the middle of a gruelling schedule of solo concerts, eleven of them in Europe. They were billed as extended improvisations, not variations on something already composed; Jarrett's intention was to create everything he played from scratch. He'd given one of these performances a night or so earlier in Switzerland, and 24 January was supposed to be an evening off. But an opportunity came up for a late-night concert in Cologne and Jarrett agreed to do it.

Jarrett was understandably particular about the pianos he performed on. For this concert, he specified a full-sized concert grand. But when he arrived at the Cologne Opera House, he found an inferior substitute: a small, out-of-tune instrument which was barely playable. Jarrett was livid and almost cancelled the concert. But more than 1,400 tickets had already been sold, and he reluctantly agreed to go ahead. By then, Jarrett was in poor shape. Exhausted by his punishing schedule, tired from travelling, wearing a brace for severe back pain and faced with an instrument he hated, everything seemed to be going wrong.

Finally, the audience took their seats, ushered in by four notes of the Opera's intermission bell. When Jarrett walked onto the stage and sat down at the piano, the first notes he played seemed oddly familiar. They were the notes of the intermission bell, and he used them as his starting point for improvisation – his way into his playing. Listen very carefully to the recording and you can hear the audience chuckle in recognition.

Then, for over an hour, Jarrett held that audience spellbound as he spun the most remarkable web of expressive musical ideas into a coherent, and deeply moving, piece – all the while grappling with that second-rate, under-powered piano. He had to adapt his usual technique to its idiosyncrasies, making it reach the gallery by pounding the keys much harder than he normally would. Technically, as well as musically, he surpassed himself. Somehow all those challenges resulted in something magical. The recording of the Köln Concert became one of the most successful albums in jazz history, selling over three million copies.

Jarrett's remarkable performance captures the essence of being expert. He had decades of study, practice and experience in performing. He had specialized in improvising musically. But on that occasion in Cologne, he did something even more remarkable. He responded to a unique situation, to the stresses of ill health and tiredness, to the inadequacies of the piano and his irritation at finding his requests ignored. Instead of narrowing his attentional focus, he widened it, even to the point of noticing and incorporating the four notes of the intermission bell. To me, that's improvisation of the highest order – an example of true mastery.

Improvisation and performance

Improvisation and performance are inseparable. Yet the word 'performance' makes many people uneasy. To them, it sounds like doing something that isn't real, that is somehow inauthentic – even faking it. I disagree radically. After all, nobody criticizes a pianist for giving a performance of a Beethoven concerto, something they have spent years studying and practising for.

Performance doesn't only happen on a stage. We talk about performing operations, performing procedures and performing experiments, as well as performing concertos and plays. For a musician, an actor or a dancer, performance is what it's all about. But it is just as important in medicine and science. And improvisation is an essential part of any performance.

Improvising is how you apply what you have learned, creating solutions in the moment and responding to what is happening around you. Yet the idea of improvisation, like the idea of performance, often unsettles people. It sounds unprofessional, a solution knocked up on the spur of the moment, like an improvised bookshelf made with a plank and some bricks or an improvised shelter in the rain. But I think it's a priceless skill. That shelter in the rain may have been jury-rigged, but it keeps you dry.

In medicine, improvisation is actually the norm. As a clinician, you're never *not* having to improvise. You're always applying existing knowledge in new contexts – because you're working with people, every situation is different. There's no such thing as a 'standard' case of pneumonia or a 'regular' stabbed neck. Each time, you're dealing with a unique human being. Even when you treat the same person for the same complaint on different occasions, it's a different situation each time. You can never step into the same river twice. You and the river have both changed.

How you improvise is key to becoming expert. It's part of your voice, your style, the way you interact with others. It's how people recognize you for the individual expert you are turning into.

Improvisation as recovery

Every so often a spectacular recovery hits the media. In January 2009, Captain Chesley Sullenberger was piloting US Airways Flight 1549, an Airbus A320 passenger plane. Soon after take-off from LaGuardia Airport in New York, the aeroplane suffered a bird strike from a flock of Canada geese. Both engines failed. In one of the most celebrated emergency landings in aviation history, Sullenberger realized he couldn't reach any nearby airports and decided to 'ditch' the plane, bringing it down on the Hudson River. Miraculously, everyone on board survived.

Talking about it afterwards, Sullenberger described how he'd dealt with the situation. Once he had made the decision to ditch, he eliminated distractions by shutting off the radio. Then he gave all his attention to bringing the plane down on water. Like all pilots, he had been training throughout his career for low-probability, high-severity events like this. It also turned out that in the phase of doing time, Sullenberger had other relevant experience, including landing seaplanes. Afterwards, he summarized his achievement like this: 'One way of looking at this might be that, for forty-two years, I've been making small, regular deposits in this bank of experience, education and training. And on January 15, the balance was sufficient so that I could make a very large withdrawal.' Despite his modesty, I think that's a perfect way of putting it.

Sullenberger's forty-two years of experience allowed him to develop a cumulative knowledge he could draw on at very short notice. When the birds struck, he brought into play those years of doing time, using his senses and working with others. He had the experience to frame the problem and decide on the best option, then create the conditions where he could give his undivided attention to bringing the airliner down on the river. He minimized extraneous demands on his attention, then used his full capacity to focus on the task and achieve the best possible chance of success.

But it's not just in aviation that such spectacular recoveries happen. In 1997, the Portuguese pianist Maria João Pires sat down to play a Mozart piano concerto at a lunchtime concert at the Concertgebouw in Amsterdam, conducted by Riccardo Chailly. As the orchestra started the opening bars, Pires realized they were playing a different concerto from the one she had prepared.

In the documentary of this extraordinary event, we see Pires in a state of shock. Chailly looks at her from the rostrum, and she tells him, 'I had another concerto in my schedule.' First he reassures her: 'You played this one last season.' Then he smiles and says, 'I'm sure you can do it – and you can do it well.'

And she does.

She gathers herself together while the orchestra finishes the introduction, then gives a flawless performance of Mozart's D minor masterpiece.

Like the bass player at the beginning of this chapter, Pires was able to improvise a solution to her daunting challenge. She had already internalized the D minor concerto and had played it many times before. But being able to reconfigure that knowledge and bring it into play with less than a minute's notice – in public, when the performance had already started – seems extraordinary. Only an expert could do that.

Being expert is not only about becoming good at your core work. It's about being able to respond to things you've never encountered, and having the confidence to go with the decisions you make. Chailly's support played a crucial role in Pires's ability to respond. Like Sullenberger, she was able to save what could have been a disastrous situation with a combination of quick thinking, experience, and a lifetime's hard work and preparation. Somehow, she was able to push away her fear and rely on the skills she had developed over decades.

Few examples of recovery are as dramatic as Sullenberger's and Pires's, but they often have similar characteristics. When Fabrice the stylist cut his client's hair too short as we saw in Chapter 6, he had to read her state of mind as he decided how to cope with the situation. Much later in his career, one of his roles was to deal with clients when another stylist had made a mistake. Partly this was because of his technical expertise in putting errors right. Even more important, though, was his ability to establish a rapport with a dissatisfied client and come up with a solution that defused the situation and led to a positive outcome.

In all these examples, skill was necessary but not sufficient. How these experts handled their own response and their relationships with other people was key. Sullenberger had to subdue his anxiety and instil confidence in his team by his comportment, while using his skill to land that huge airliner on a river. Pires had to work with Chailly and the orchestra to create an unforgettable experience for the audience. Fabrice had to put himself in his client's position, addressing her concerns without becoming defensive. All of them wanted to achieve the best possible result under circumstances they couldn't have predicted.

'Yes, and . . .'

So far, I've talked about improvisation in a general sense – as the ability to respond to what's around you and come up with solutions to the challenges you find. In theatre, the word 'improvisation' has a more specialized meaning.

In 1979, the theatre director Keith Johnstone published *Impro*, in which he describes his work with groups of actors. For Johnstone, improvisation is a skill that can be studied and practised, underpinned by a cardinal principle: it depends on willingness by all concerned – willingness to listen, willingness to respond, and willingness to work together in a creative rather than a destructive way. If a pair of actors was improvising a sketch, Johnstone would insist that every response should start with 'Yes, *and*. . .', building on the other's move and opening up new possibilities. This is the opposite of the 'Yes, *but*. . .' response, which blocks the next move and shuts down possibilities. Johnstone would ask participants to come with a calm mind, prepared to draw on whatever was inside them for the good of the joint performance.

This is far more difficult than it sounds. We are so used to our internal critic making judgements about what is likely to work – and what isn't – that it can be difficult to let go. But this willingness to accept and respond to what another person offers is central to becoming expert. It's another aspect of 'it's not about you, it's about them'. It shows respect for the perspectives of other people, whether you're an actor or a doctor.

Up to this point in the path to becoming expert, you've been conforming to the framework you have chosen to work in. Your reference point has been the work as it is already done. You copy others, do things as they do. You remain within a system. But now you are questioning the system and redefining its limits. You are using your individuality to do what you think is best. No longer compelled to stick to how other people do things, the onus is on you to do them in the best way you can.

Sometimes this need to think differently is forced upon you, as when I was operating on Themba and his stabbed neck. I didn't want to move outside the system I'd learned, but at that moment the system wasn't working. I had to do something, and what I'd learned didn't help. When you're out of your depth, you have to think for yourself or something bad will happen.

In the performing arts, improvisation isn't the exclusive province of jazz or theatre. Far from it. Improvisation in classical music was highly prized for centuries. The ability to sway the ear in gentle undulation, to use C. P. E. Bach's words, was all about responding to the moment and adapting your performance accordingly. Now there is a resurgence of interest in this concept. David Dolan, Professor of Classical Improvisation at London's Guildhall School of Music and Drama, explained it to me like this: 'Until a little over a century ago, all musicians were expected to include improvisational elements in their performances. Every time they played a repeat passage it would be different. Now, they are assessed on how closely they stick to what is written; how "accurately" they play the notes, rhythm and dynamics specified on the page. That squeezes out their ability to improvise.' For Dolan, the true art is to fully internalize the structure of the music you're playing, then use it as a point of departure you return to as you create fresh interpretations of what you already know. It made me think of Bill Evans the jazz pianist, alone in his garage, analysing his technique for month after painstaking month.

There is a world of difference between playing the notes 'correctly' – that is to say, as written – and playing them as you want them to be heard. As a musician, you are not re-enacting something you've practised and perfected in isolation, but entering a dialogue. A piece of music only comes to life when you go beyond what is written on the page, when you breathe your personality into it as you're playing.

It's the same with any performance. To do it well, you have to understand the underlying structure, the essential architecture of your work. When you perform, you are connecting that structure with your own emotional world and that of your audience. Magicians, for instance, have to deal with the occasional slip of a finger, or cope with an audience member who forgets which card they chose. There's always an element of unpredictability in performance, always the need to bring your skills together in the moment.

Of course, there is a difference between the improvisational flexibility that brings a piece of written music to life during performance, and the improvisation that happens independently of existing repertoire. But in both forms you have to remain alert, to listen attentively to what is happening around you, and always respond with Johnstone's 'Yes, *and* . . .'

Just like playing jazz, being a doctor depends on improvisation, especially if you're a GP. Each encounter with a patient is unique and unpredictable, yet it takes place within a canon of medical knowledge and skill you've spent years acquiring – your equivalent of a trumpet player's scales and techniques. This canon provides a safety net which gives you the freedom to go in unexpected directions. As an inexperienced clinician, you may be reluctant to start a conversation that could lead into areas you don't feel competent to deal with, or to move outside your textbook knowledge. Later on, you develop the confidence to ask different questions, to probe a little, to risk discomfort. If you try to force a consultation to stay within rigid lines, patients will feel frog-marched. You may be responding to what you want the problem to be because you know how to treat it, rather than finding out what that problem actually is. Instead, you have to listen carefully, then take each part of the conversation forward with a 'Yes, *and* . . .' This means taking risks.

Those skills you built up through doing time, becoming familiar with the materiality of your craft, and learning to recognize the nature of thin materials and their imminent collapse – all these have to be present. You can't improvise without them. But you don't have to show them. The more expert the expert, the less you see what they've had to do to get there. As Bill Evans the jazz icon pointed out and we saw in the previous chapter, the danger comes if a learner tries to mimic what an expert does without having gone through those years of graft. In medicine, for example, you can easily mistake the smoothness of an expert's improvised performance for a cosy chat. You might think you could do that too. Very soon, you would find you can't.

The workmanship of risk

Joshua the tailor is an expert improviser, a master of the unexpected. Soon after he set up as an independent tailor, he took on a customer who didn't know what he wanted. Joshua said something like this: 'If you let me design and make you a jacket, I can't tell you exactly what it will look like or even how long it will take. But I can tell you it will be the best jacket you've ever had.'

Many people would have felt uneasy at that point, but this client was willing to go with it. Joshua was as good as his word, the jacket was superb and the customer loved it. Part of that contract involved a willingness by both parties to live with uncertainty while the jacket was being made. It's what David Pye was talking about when he contrasted the workmanship of certainty and the workmanship of risk. I have found this a useful distinction, but it needs some explanation.

Pye was a well-known furniture-maker and Professor of Furniture Design at the Royal College of Art in

London. In 1968, he published his influential book *The Nature and Art of Workmanship*. He begins with a definition:

> If I must ascribe a meaning to the word craftsmanship, I shall say as a first approximation that it means simply workmanship using any kind of technique or apparatus, in which the quality of the result is not predetermined, but depends on the judgement, dexterity and care which the maker exercises as he works. The essential idea is that the quality of the result is continually at risk during the process of making; and so I shall call this kind of workmanship 'The workmanship of risk': an uncouth phrase but at least descriptive.
>
> It may be mentioned in passing that in workmanship the care counts for more than the judgement and dexterity; though care may well become habitual and unconscious.

Pye goes on:

> With the workmanship of risk we may contrast the workmanship of certainty, always to be found in quantity production, and found in its pure state in full automation. In workmanship of this sort the quality of the result is exactly predetermined before a single saleable thing is made . . . The most typical and familiar example of the workmanship of risk is writing with a pen, and of the workmanship of certainty, modern printing . . . in principle the distinction between the

two different kinds of workmanship is clear and turns on the question: 'Is the result predetermined and unalterable once production begins?'

Pye's example from the 1960s may seem odd to modern readers, when handwriting is in decline and printing has become digital. Nevertheless, his point is clear. His emphasis on 'any kind of technique or apparatus' shows that he is not thinking only of traditional techniques of making, but is looking ahead to new technologies as they emerge. And Pye is not talking of the risk of poor quality. Instead he is talking about inherent uncertainty, the inability to specify in advance exactly what will happen. The risk is to the predictability of the result, not to those using or experiencing it.

All the experts I describe in this book deal in the workmanship of risk. A surgical operation, a bespoke suit, a clinical consultation, a magic show, a stone carving, a musical performance, a hairstyle – the result is not predetermined and unalterable in any of them. They all contain uncertainty.

To the modern reader, the word 'risk' has other resonances, suggesting the probability of danger to ourselves or others, of financial consequences or threats to public safety. Of course, the two notions of risk overlap, especially when human beings are concerned. When working with people, nothing can ever be certain. Thus Pye highlights judgement, dexterity and care, with care counting for more than the other two.

For all his old-fashioned terminology, Pye's ideas ring true to me – and he crystallizes something crucial. A necessary uncertainty runs through expert work. As you gain experience, you have to accept and deal with that. That's why the ability to improvise, to come up with new solutions, is critical. As a surgeon, I came to realize that all I could know for certain before starting an operation was that there were things I couldn't know in advance. It might be the details of the injury or the presence of an anatomical variation. It might be how that patient's organs and tissues would behave, or how they would hold sutures. It might be how much bleeding I'd encounter, how tissue planes might be stuck down or obliterated because of previous surgery or infection. I couldn't tell beforehand which structures would be thin materials on the verge of collapse.

It was during this not-knowing that I needed the confidence and the skill that would allow me to improvise. I might not be able to tell in advance what I was going to find, but I had to feel I could deal with it.

Responding to the unpredictable

Improvisation and risk go hand in hand. When you try something new, there's always the possibility that it won't work out the way you hoped. In Chapter 6, we looked at what happens when you get things wrong and have to put them right. In this chapter, we've explored the idea that experts are always improvising, always responding to the unexpected. Now, we'll bring these ideas together to talk about resilience and recovery.

Experts take responsibility for the variation inherent in their work. They read the materials they work with and the people their work is for – their audience, their clients, their patients. Experts adapt their knowhow to each set of circumstances, and reconsider the problem every time. They remain in dialogue with their work and their audience. Dealing with complications goes with the territory, and learning how to cope when things go wrong is one of the marks of becoming expert. Resilience and recovery are essential qualities if you are to continue to develop as an expert.

Sometimes a bowel anastomosis (joining two sections of intestine together after cutting a section out) springs a leak after the operation itself is over. These things happen and it's nobody's fault. In medicine, they are referred to as 'complications'. They're part of the uncertainty that goes with operating; some patients heal better than others.

This is different from making an error. Complications are things that go wrong even when you have done the right thing. Every surgical operation has a complication rate, and you can give it a number. You might say that the leakage rate after partial gastrectomy (removing part of the stomach) is 5 per cent. If you operate on one hundred patients, five of them will have a leak. When that happens to someone you've operated on, it doesn't necessarily mean you did anything wrong, though it's hard to believe that at the time. It's just one of the realities of working with live human beings.

There are equivalents in every field. If you're a ceramicist, there's an inherent unpredictability about glazing and firing. Sometimes a batch simply doesn't work and you can't figure out why. If you haven't ever had a complication, it usually just means you haven't done enough operations, made enough pots or been working in your field for long enough.

We often think of the tangible things which experts create, like vases, paintings or suits. But, as we've seen, many experts create transient experiences such as music, magic or fine dining. Here, too, there is the workmanship of risk. Here, too, there is uncertainty.

Doing the best job you can means doing things slightly differently each time, responding to the specifics of the moment. Whenever that happens, you have improvised. When Joshua says, 'This will be the best jacket you have ever had,' he is asking his customer to trust him to come up with a solution for their unique needs, rather than applying a predetermined approach. Joshua's skill, like mine as a GP, lies as much in defining the problem as in knowing how to solve it. This highlights the contrast between a human expert and an algorithm. Some medical procedures, such as diagnosing cervical cancer by identifying abnormal smear cells under the microscope, can be done effectively by mechanized systems. But robots are no good at telling patients that they have cancer or listening to their concerns. Each doctor will approach a diagnosis differently, judging what's best for that patient.

Learning to sit on your hands

A lot of published research compares surgery to aviation, exploring how cockpit drills can make surgical procedures safer. By introducing systems from the flight deck, the argument goes, it should be possible to eliminate errors like putting in a heart valve the wrong way round. But now that flying is so safe, most civil aviation has become routine and uneventful. On long-haul international flights, very little happens for much of the time. Of course, there is still extensive training for every conceivable contingency. As we saw when Captain Chesley Sullenberger had to bring his airliner down on the Hudson River, every so often a major disaster occurs – or is narrowly avoided. But these are rare exceptions. Military aviation is a different story.

Phil Bayman is a combat pilot. With over 4,500 flying hours in his logbook, he has seen pretty much everything. Not only has he flown countless missions, but he also trains other pilots. Many of the Red Arrows (the crack UK aerobatic team) are his former students.

Phil and his colleagues have been through all the steps in this book. By the time a combat pilot starts going out on operational sorties, only 15 per cent of their attentional capacity is taken up by flying the plane. The remaining 85 per cent is 'mission management', assessing and responding to each situation and making split-second decisions. When you think that Hawks and Tornadoes fly at near-supersonic speeds, you begin to realize what these pilots face. As Phil puts it, 'You are at the limits of your capability.'

Combat flying makes extraordinary demands. In addition to external threats like enemy aircraft, missiles and the challenges of terrain and weather, there are physiological hazards such as G-forces. Phil explained it to me like this: 'Combat flying is a big game of chess and there are many, many variables. If something starts to go wrong – with your plane, your body or your team – you have to decide which is the biggest crocodile trying to clamber into your boat, and deal with that first.' To do so, you need to keep your wits about you, to respond to what's happening around and within you – in other words, to improvise.

Improvising is a skill you can learn. Phil has a mantra for the pilots he teaches: 'When things go wrong – sit on your hands and count to ten. There's very little that can't wait for a short time. There are bigger dangers in acting too soon, in committing yourself to a line of action you haven't thought through.' Despite the obvious differences between piloting a fighter jet in a dogfight at the speed of sound and leading a surgical operation, his approach makes perfect sense to me as a clinician.

As a trauma surgeon, you have to decide which are

the biggest crocodiles trying to clamber into your boat. When you're faced with torrential bleeding, your first impulse is to put a clamp on something. But in that pool of blood you might clamp the wrong thing and make matters worse. Surgical textbooks describe techniques for gaining control, for recognizing where the blood is coming from, for repairing arteries and veins. They say much less about your internal state – about what it *feels* like to be on the front line during an operation. It's not just the bleeding, it's how you respond that determines the outcome. Experienced surgeons have learned to gain temporary control of a situation before making irrevocable decisions. They might put in gauze packs and press hard, controlling the bleeding for long enough to step back, think through the options and decide on a strategy. Figuratively speaking, they, too, sit on their hands and count to ten.

Surgery has its G-force equivalents. Tiredness is one of them. During my training it took me a long time to recognize that my decision-making towards the end of a weekend on call, sleep-deprived after working for forty-eight hours non-stop, was questionable to say the least. Gradually I began to understand the signs. I would start to slow down, become indecisive, giggle inappropriately, and become unable to process multiple sources of information. Like pilots experiencing severe G-forces, these manifestations of fatigue are insidious. They creep up without you noticing.

In the operating theatre that evening with Themba, I

was lucky. It was early in the intake and I was fully alert. In that welter of blood, I pulled myself together and tried to be methodical, identifying landmarks so I could orient myself and work out what had been injured. My assistant dabbed gently with a swab and suddenly a jet of blood spurted out. Pulsatile, so it must be arterial. Sister Mbata handed me a gauze pack; I fed it into the wound and got my assistant to press hard while I gathered myself and tried to think logically. At least I'd stabilized things for long enough to fight my panic and consider my options. I'd reached a place of temporary safety where I could pause and reset. Knowing how to find that place of safety was crucial.

Finding your place of safety

Why is sitting on your hands important? And what does it have to do with improvisation? Improvisation requires you to notice cues and respond to them. When you're dealing with an emergency, or when you're tired or stressed out, your attention narrows to a single point. Having a method to reach a place of safety, kicking the biggest crocodile out of your boat, allows you to experiment and improvise a more permanent solution – to sail somewhere where there aren't any crocodiles.

Long after my experience with Themba, I invited a group of experts to spend a day discussing error and recovery. Phil Bayman the combat pilot was one of them.

He set the scene by telling us about an occasion when something felt wrong as he was coming in to land, though he didn't know what. He'd gone through all the steps of his pre-landing checklist, but he still had a sense that something felt odd. Instead of trying to analyse the problem, he aborted his landing, put on full power and climbed to a safe altitude. Once he had time to think, he realized that, despite going through his checklist, he hadn't actually pulled the lever that activated the undercarriage. He had said the words, but he hadn't done the action, just like my student doctor who had gone through the motions of taking somebody's pulse without actually counting it. Unlike the student, though, Phil the expert recognized when something was wrong. In that moment, he only had seconds to react; if he'd stopped to analyse the situation, he'd have crashed and died. By responding instinctively and climbing to a place of safety, he bought himself time. Only when things were more stable did he replay the last few minutes in his mind and identify the problem.

Though the experts in this book work in very different fields, they have all developed a feeling for what the embroiderer Fleur Oakes refers to as 'wrongness', a special sense that puts them on high alert. When that occurs they do something about it, often so fast that they hardly know what's happened. They have developed systems which stabilize the situation, then give them time to analyse the problem and work out what to do – allowing them to sit on their hands and count to ten. That's how they can switch from forward-thinking reasoning, where they just do what works, to backward-thinking reasoning about the cause.

Not all problems happen with the intensity of combat flying, of course. Earlier in his career, Joshua sometimes had trouble with fitting a sleeve to a jacket. Usually this went smoothly, but sometimes he would realize that things were not going according to plan. The sleeve didn't seem to fit and everything became a struggle. At first he would fiddle with the fabric, but that only made things worse and he would feel his hands tensing up. Eventually he learned to use that tenseness as a signal that it was time to put the work aside and think differently. He would stop sewing and make a cup of tea. That was his place of safety. When he came back, the problem looked different. Once the situation was stabilized, he could think back to those fundamental principles of construction his teacher had taught him. That allowed him to analyse the problem, bring his backward-thinking reasoning into play and then improvise. But first he had to pause, reset and consider.

One of my surgical consultants said almost the same thing when I was starting my training at Baragwanath. 'If the shit hits the fan and you don't know what to do,' she told me, 'start by doing nothing. Call for some gauze packs, get your assistant to press hard, then go and have a cup of tea. By the time you come back and re-scrub, things will look different.' I didn't believe her at first, but in that operating theatre with Themba, her words came back to me.

In one sense, the challenges I've just described could hardly be more different. Nobody dies if you play a wrong note or bungle a sleeve, whereas you could easily be wiped out in a fighter aircraft or severely damage a patient on the operating table. But the principle of recognizing that something isn't right, going to a place of safety and thinking what to do next is a characteristic of the expert improviser.

When novices narrow their focus, experts widen theirs. They respond to the situation as a whole, not to isolated elements. Sometimes a completely different solution pops into their mind. Sometimes they experience serendipity.

Turning wrong into right

Katharine Coleman is a glass engraver, widely known for her exquisite work with coloured glass. She depends on expert glassblowers to create the materials she works with. One day, Katharine collected a heavy bowl she was going to engrave as a commission. She was shocked to notice that there were ash marks in the glass. Horrified, she complained to the glassblower. He looked at her pityingly, then reassured her that the marks were just on the surface and everything would be fine. Just polish it, he told her, and the marks would disappear.

Katharine didn't believe him. She couldn't see or feel

anything on the surface, and she was convinced that the glass itself was faulty. Back in her studio she examined the bowl again, even more sure that ash from the making process had been embedded in it. But she had no alternative, so she polished it anyway. To her astonishment, within a few seconds all the marks had vanished. Just as the glassblower had told her, the ash had been on the surface all along, and it was the optical properties of the curved bowl that made it look internal.

Katharine's first feeling was overwhelming relief. But with a flash of insight, she realized she had stumbled on something that could revolutionize her practice. Anything you do on the outer surface of a thick-walled piece of curved glass looks different once it's been refracted by the transparent material and reflected onto its inner surface. Though glassblowers have known this since time immemorial, it needed someone like Katharine to exploit the phenomenon for engraving. Now, working to Katharine's specification, the glassblower covers a thick-walled transparent bowl with a thin skin of coloured glass, like the peel of an apple or a potato. Katharine uses this like a canvas for incising her designs, allowing her to develop the creations she is now widely known for.

Katharine told me she could easily have focused on being angry that the glass she had ordered had gone wrong (as she thought). But instead she reframed that experience as an opportunity. From this point of view, error, variation and unpredictability are not to be eliminated. They are to be embraced, because they spur creativity – if you have the imagination to see it like that. That sort of imagination is a form of improvisation, of recognizing the potential within an unexpected situation. Like Keith Johnstone and his actors, Katharine was responding with 'Yes, *and* . . .'

Improvising under pressure

In the operating theatre at Bara with Themba, I'm fighting a rising sense of panic. My assistant suppresses the bleeding with a gauze pack, and I have time to get some distance. I walk round the operating theatre, trying to calm down and think. Back at the table, I remove the pack and discover that the knife wound has gone through a branch of Themba's carotid artery. I clip and tie it, hoping that will solve the problem. It doesn't, and blood continues to spurt. It's coming from the back of his neck and I realize it must be the vertebral artery. This is a *nightmare* scenario. As its name suggests, the artery runs through a bony channel formed by the cervical vertebrae. This makes it almost inaccessible. Arteries are elastic, and if one has been severed, its cut ends retract. If that happens inside a place where you can't reach it, such as that bony channel in the neck, the blood will keep pumping and the patient may bleed to death in front of you. I've already seen that happen more than once.

With Themba, nobody else is available to help. Even

if I call my consultant in from home it will be at least forty-five minutes before she arrives, and by then it may be too late. It's up to me to do something, and do it now. I'm scared stiff, I'm not yet an expert and I'm seriously out of my depth. But I have to put that to one side. Now I really have to improvise. I try to think as widely as I can. I need inspiration.

Suddenly I have a brainwave. From somewhere – maybe a coffee-room conversation, or an operative surgery book, a journal or just someone's anecdote – I remember a story about using the balloon of a Foley catheter to control this kind of bleeding. Foley catheters are usually used for draining urine. You feed one along a patient's urethra until the catheter's tip is in the bladder. Then you use a syringe to inflate a tiny balloon that stops the catheter slipping out again. The idea with a vertebral artery injury is that the bony channel is so narrow that even a small balloon will apply enough pressure to stop the artery spurting blood. This 'tamponade', as it's called, can be a lifesaver. At least, that's the theory. It's worth a try. I've got to do something, as Themba's in danger of bleeding out.

I take a deep breath and ask for a paediatric Foley catheter. Sister Mbata looks at me as if I've gone loopy – we're operating on an adult's neck, not a child's pelvis. But she gets me one anyway. Although she has no idea what I'm trying to do, she responds to my weird request with a 'Yes, *and* . . .' We are improvising together.

I feed the catheter into the depths of Themba's wound.

Every time I move the gauze swab, the field fills up with blood. Finally, I manoeuvre the catheter's tip into position, inflate the balloon and cross my fingers. Mercifully the bleeding stops and Themba's blood pressure stabilizes. Things are under control at last, and I can take my time. It's still difficult, but finally I get a clip on the artery and stop the blood flooding out. Things are more straightforward from then on and I go back to the techniques I've learned from books. An hour or so later it's almost over, and I'm closing the skin. Themba's lost a lot of blood and he needs to go to the intensive care unit, but he's young and fit. He makes a good recovery, and soon he's able to go back to the general ward. Not long after that, he's well enough to go home. But it was a close call.

My experience that night in the operating theatre with Themba turned out to be a watershed. Watching him leave hospital a few days after I feared he'd die on the operating table showed me yet again that not everything I needed to know was in the books. It gave me the confidence that I could find a solution when I needed to. Decades later, my heart still races when I think back to that operation. At the time I was just thankful to have got away with it, to have come up with a trick that worked. But now I think of it as improvisation, of drawing on information that was floating around somewhere in my mind – finding it when I needed it most. At last, I was beginning to become expert.

The ability to improvise is characteristic of any expert.

It's how people bring together the skills and insights they've been developing for years and apply them to each new situation they encounter. Like the bass player in the jazz trio earlier in this chapter, you're able to solve a problem you couldn't have anticipated. Sometimes, this capacity to think round corners can even take your work in a new direction. That's what the next chapter is about.

APPRENTICE   JOURNEYMAN   **MASTER**

PASSING
IT ON

'IT'S NOT
ABOUT YOU'

DOING
TIME

USING YOUR
SENSES

DEVELOPING
VOICE

SPACE AND
OTHER PEOPLE

10. Changing direction

It's September 2014 and I'm at the Art Workers' Guild in London, that remarkable organization I described in Chapter 1. We're about to begin an all-day event I've called 'Thread Management'. I've brought together a group of experts who all work with threads. Several of them, like me, are surgeons. One's a vascular consultant who operates on arteries and veins. Another is a cardiac surgeon who specializes in repairing diseased heart valves, rather than replacing them. A third's a paediatric surgeon, used to working on babies and children. Another is a scrub nurse, a key part of any surgical team.

Alongside the surgeons we've got experts from outside medicine. I've invited three puppeteers, who use threads to bring their marionettes to life. There's a fisherman, who uses lines for casting and tying flies for catching trout. There's one of the UK's leading experts in experimental knitting and textile design. And there are a couple of engineers from Imperial, who are analysing threads mathematically to create computer models.

We're all here because of Fleur Oakes, the three-dimensional embroiderer whose ideas of 'wrongness' came up in Chapter 9. Fleur had come to a surgical simulation I led that had demonstrated how surgeons join segments of intestine using sutures. For me, the focus had been on showing how the team created an anastomosis in gut or blood vessels, something I'd done countless times as a trauma surgeon. But when Fleur saw that simulation, she wasn't interested in anatomy, or the nuances of injury or disease. What she saw was how the surgical team used sutures and needles. She called it 'thread management'.

Fleur's never been to medical school. Instead, she studied fine art, fashion design and embroidery. She's an expert maker, and an expert teacher too. When I asked her what she meant by 'thread management', she said, 'I noticed you'd got all these threads floating around during that operation. That's what happens with my students too. The first thing I have to teach them is how not to get their threads tangled up. I tell them that a thread should never be longer than the distance from your fingers to your elbow; that you have to pay constant attention to each thread's tension; that you have to make sure the thread doesn't twist up in a spiral like an old-fashioned telephone cable if you're sewing along a curve.'

I wish someone had said that to me when I was training in surgery. As an assistant, I lost count of the number of times I allowed a thread to get snarled up in a retractor while I was 'following' my boss as she completed a difficult anastomosis. As a surgeon myself, I often got frustrated by the way fine suture material twisted up in a spiral when I was sewing along a curve.

I'd learned my sewing from the surgeons I worked for. I never thought that an embroiderer might be able to help, because I never thought about professional embroiderers at all. At the time I hardly knew they existed. Years later, when Fleur made her comment about thread management, I realized she'd seen something in surgery that had been there all the time but I'd never noticed. She saw thread as a focal point. So we decided to explore this idea with other experts.

That day at the Art Workers' Guild took Fleur's work and mine in new directions. We'd asked all the participants to bring examples of their work and the materials they use. The surgeons and scrub nurse brought instruments, sutures and models of arteries. The fisherman had his rod and line; the puppeteers brought a bag full of marionettes; the textile artist had her spinning wheel; and the mathematicians brought a computer with their modelling software. Seeing these experts demonstrate their skills showed me that looking outside my own field could shine new light on what I thought I knew. Since then, cross-disciplinary exploration has become the focus of my research.

Thread Management transformed things for Fleur too, opening up a new phase in her career. At that event at the Art Workers' Guild, she found herself sitting next to Colin Bicknell, a consultant vascular surgeon. Fleur and Colin hit it off at once. Fleur had brought an embroidery frame and Colin had brought a simulated aorta made of silicon. When Colin demonstrated how he replaced a diseased aortic segment, inserting a Dacron graft with tiny stitches, Fleur immediately felt at home. Her own work with stitches seemed weirdly similar, even though the purpose was completely different.

Colin invited Fleur into his theatre to watch him operate on real patients, and she's never looked back. For over three years, she's been the embroiderer-in-residence in Colin's vascular surgery unit, a role that is probably unique. She's spent countless hours watching Colin and his team, figuring out how to use her skills to help trainee surgeons with theirs. She's watched the surgeons deal with everything you can imagine, from blocked leg arteries to ruptured aortic aneurysms that can kill in minutes. But she hasn't just confined their work to Colin's world. She's invited him and his students to her studio in north London, teaching them how to look, to draw and to sew like artists. She's designed a training programme for helping surgeons build their skills, starting with simple exercises in knotting and embroidery before progressing to complex procedures on fragile vintage fabrics which fall to pieces at a touch. It's uncannily like operating on sick patients whose arteries are as soft as butter or as brittle as clay pipes.

Fleur makes sense of what she sees in Colin's operating theatre because she's already an expert. Let's explore what's happening here in terms of the path in this book.

Fleur has been through all the stages I've described

so far. She spent years at art school, studying to become a dressmaker as well as a fashion designer – doing time and learning to use her senses. She set up her own fashion house, designing and producing garments for other people. She got things wrong and had to put them right. In her fashion house she learned to recognize what her customers wanted, creating designs that matched their needs. Like the other experts in this book, she had to make the transition to 'it's not about you' and she developed her voice.

The 2008 economic crash demolished Fleur's business, so for a while she morphed into a bespoke corset maker, creating a niche which brought together her talents as a designer and as a maker. She didn't abandon the skills she had learned, but turned them into something else. In terms of the previous chapter, she *improvised*. But although she was good at corset-making, she realized she wasn't cut out for it. She wanted a challenge that made full use of her dexterity and imagination. So, inspired by historic costumes in London's Victoria and Albert Museum, she became fascinated with three-dimensional embroidery. She spent hours recreating Jacobean stumpwork, working at a microscopic scale to create embroidered shapes based on the natural world. Now she's one of the leading experts in this unusual field.

By this time, Fleur was becoming well known, and highly respected as a craftsman and a teacher. She could have gone on doing that for the rest of her career. But in becoming the embroiderer-in-residence at

Colin Bicknell's vascular surgery unit, Fleur has taken a new direction. Instead of carrying on as she was in the field she trained in, she's redefining it.

Not many experts do this. Most continue along the path they chose at the beginning. Having gone through the Apprentice phase in someone else's workshop, then honing and refining their expertise as Journeymen, they become Masters. They focus on passing on their knowledge to those who are following the path they themselves trod. This is vital work, not only for the learners who come up through the system, but for the survival of the system itself.

Experts like these continue their work in the way they have learned it. Clinicians look after patients in much the same way as their teachers, even though they take on new techniques. Magicians do magic shows, staying within a well-established way of working while developing new tricks or routines. Bespoke tailors continue making suits based on patterns and blocks that have been handed down through generations.

But some experts strike out in a different direction. These people challenge the nature of their field. Some, like Fleur, find inspiration in an unfamiliar setting that prompts them to think in new ways and from unexpected perspectives. Others, like John Wickham the keyhole surgery pioneer, revolutionize their whole field. These are the ones we'll explore in this chapter. I'll start with Mr Wickham.

Pioneers of keyhole surgery

If you have your gallbladder removed these days, it will almost certainly be done by keyhole surgery. You'll have a couple of tiny incisions in your abdomen, be out of hospital the same day and back to work soon after. But it wasn't always like that. When I was training as a surgeon in the 1980s, patients would be in hospital for weeks after elective surgery for gallstones. They'd have large painful wounds that took ages to heal. The procedure I was taught had been standard practice for decades. An educational film from the 1920s shows an operation almost identical to the one I learned as a surgical registrar. Then, almost overnight, everything changed.

The introduction of keyhole surgery in the late 1980s didn't tinker round the edges of what was already there. It was a revolution which turned surgery on its head, and a key figure in that revolution was Mr John Wickham. John died in October 2017 at the age of eighty-nine. He was one of the world's leading surgical pioneers, and a lifelong innovator.

After pioneering minimally invasive ('keyhole') surgery in the 1980s, he continued to disrupt the medical world. He invented countless new technologies, including one of the first robot-assisted systems for removing the prostate. His ideas reverberate to this day, though until recently his contribution has been unjustly overlooked. I got to know John and his colleagues in the years before he died, and came to realize just how influential this gentle, soft-spoken man was.

John was a urologist. He specialized in treating patients with kidney stones. Like all the experts in this book, he went through the stages of Apprentice, Journeyman and Master. As a young trainee surgeon he gained a wide range of experience, including a spell in neurosurgery. For the first few years after he became a consultant, he performed operations which were standard at the time, making large incisions to expose the kidney and take out urinary tract stones.

He could have spent the rest of his career within this field. But John was restless, impatient with the status quo, and constantly searching for better ways to treat his patients. At first, his innovations took place within his specialty. He designed new instruments, including the Wickham retractor for open surgery which is still in use today. John was passionate about the quality of his work. In the operating theatre he tried to be as delicate with kidneys as neurosurgeons were with brains. He had a deep respect for human tissues and he carried out research into ways of operating on the kidney which minimized damage.

But John's vision went further than that. He told me that when he went to see his patients the day after their surgery, they would be in a lot of pain. An incision the length of a runner bean stretched around their side. John would hold up something the size of a lentil and say, 'We've got your stone, Mr Smith.' The size of the incision seemed out of all proportion to the tiny stone. To John, this simply didn't make sense. He began to question the need for large incisions, challenging the orthodoxies of the time. Later, he wrote, 'We still have far too many surgeons who believe that unless you cut a hole big enough to get your head in, you cannot see well enough to perform a proper operation.'

Bringing about change is never easy, and John's vision of a different kind of surgery made him unpopular with some of his colleagues. Surgery in the 1980s was very hierarchical. I know, because I was a trainee at the time and I was on the receiving end. Shit flowed downhill and I was at the bottom. But John Wickham didn't believe in hierarchies, and he wasn't interested in power or status. He wanted to create the best possible experience for the patients under his care, and he built a most unusual team. Decades later, I came to know many of them myself, when I began to research the early days of keyhole surgery.

John was in his eighties by then and many of his colleagues had also retired, but they all vividly remember that time. Toni Raybould (scrub nurse), Mike Kellett (interventional radiologist), Chris Russell (surgeon) and Stuart Greengrass (engineer and surgical instrument designer) talk about how John brought them together to find ways of minimizing the trauma inflicted by surgery. His ideas of teamwork broke new ground.

It was a heady time in surgery. Technology was moving at breakneck speed, and imaging techniques such as ultrasound and CT scanning were revolutionizing how doctors saw internal organs. Fibre-optics and miniaturization made it possible to pass tiny telescopes into body cavities. Lasers were opening up new possibilities for using energy to cure disease. The list seemed endless. With John's encouragement to take risks and be inventive, his research fellows came up with a host of new ideas. Some of these ideas turned out not to be feasible and petered out. Others, like flexible cystoscopy (using a narrow fibre-optic tube to look inside the bladder), have become standard practice.

One day, John Wickham and Mike Kellett made a breakthrough. First, Kellett manoeuvred a fine wire into their patient's kidney under X-ray control, then used dilators to create a tract big enough for a miniature telescope (a 'laparoscope') to pass. Guiding his laparoscope along the tract, John made a small incision in the kidney, grasped the stone and pulled it out. As he did so, the team burst into a spontaneous round of applause – something seldom heard in operating theatres. The patient went home after a couple of days, instead of needing weeks in hospital to recover. The team had performed the UK's first percutaneous nephrolithotomy, removing a lentil-sized kidney stone through a lentil-sized incision. It was a pivotal moment.

From then on, things moved quickly. In the years that followed, Wickham and his team shaped a field which was evolving internationally. Kellett, already renowned for his ability to visualize anatomy in three dimensions, became increasingly skilled at placing wires and tubes in apparently inaccessible parts of the body. Greengrass came up with engineering solutions to the clinical problems Wickham was facing, such as how to get the best view through a laparoscope, how to zoom in and out, and how to design instruments along ergonomic principles. Raybould integrated these new technologies into the rhythms of the operating theatre.

But John wasn't content to revolutionize his specialist field of urology. After coining the term 'minimally invasive surgery' (later popularized as 'keyhole surgery'), he realized that this approach had huge implications for surgery as a whole, though it would be several more years before it became widespread. In a prescient editorial in the *British Medical Journal* in 1987, he wrote: 'it seems extraordinary that general surgeons have not yet seized upon the potential of the laparoscope'. Only a couple of years later, the general surgeons *did* seize on that potential, changing the landscape of surgery forever. Since then, operation after operation has been transformed by keyhole surgery, and John's dream has become a reality.

Masters of innovation

Not many people can claim to have revolutionized their field in the way that John Wickham and his colleagues revolutionized mine. But many of the experts in this book have taken a similar turn away from the orthodox world they trained in. David Owen, a magician with a parallel career as a barrister, had the idea of using the skills of performing magic to help young people with disabilities. With the support of a hospital charity led by Yvonne Farquharson, David and Richard McDougall (whom we met in Chapter 7) became founding members of Breathe Arts Magic. They created two-week summer camps for children and young people with hemiplegia, a one-sided weakness of the body usually caused by birth trauma affecting the brain. Many of these young people were unable to do up their buttons or use a zip, because of their inability to coordinate basic movements. Often, they felt socially isolated, struggling at school and seen as different by their peers.

David and Richard collaborated with occupational therapists to design magic tricks that these young people would want to practise, but which would also help their coordination and build their confidence. The programme was a runaway success. The young people became hooked on magic, practising for hours after every session. As well as making coins vanish and rubber bands hop mysteriously through the air, these young performers developed confidence and social skills through engaging with an audience, using eye contact to direct the attention of those watching. As I discovered when I visited one of the summer sessions, seeing these young people performing a magic trick, then opening a bag of crisps by themselves for the first time in their lives, was an unforgettable experience.

One of the magicians in David Owen's group is Will Houstoun. He, too, has redefined his field. Although Will has been fascinated by magic for as long as he can remember, he only became a professional magician after completing a master's degree in mechanical engineering. When we met Will in Chapter 7, he was already highly successful. A winner of the European Magic Championships, he had become Magic Circle Close-up Magician of the Year 2015. He had perfected an eight-minute act, performing two shows a night, six nights a week. He had created an experience that audiences loved, making coins and playing cards wink in and out of existence. He told me he was doing what a magician was supposed to do, what other magicians wanted to see being done, and what those other magicians had decided magic ought to be. But despite having become a con-summate performer, he wasn't satisfied by magic shows alone. He wanted to create his own form of magic.

At that time, Will was just completing his PhD in the history of Victorian magic. He wanted to challenge his audiences into thinking more widely, and was interested in the relationship between truth and deception. So he developed a new form of magic show, telling stories about magicians from the past. In it, he brings these magicians to life, performing their tricks himself; but as an added twist, Will playfully calls into question the truth of the historical stories themselves.

Will described his purpose like this: 'This perform-ance may not follow the traditional pattern of a magic show, but in making structural changes I've developed the kind of show I would want to see, one which says the things about magic which I'd like to say.' Will is not conforming to what other magicians do, but reframing what it means to be a magician.

Recently, Will and I have been exploring how the skills of magic can help students of science and medicine think of their work as performance. As magician-in-residence at the Centre for Performance Science, which I lead, Will is exploring how the skills of capturing and shaping attention can help clinicians and musicians in their own professions.

Back to Fleur in Colin's operating theatre. Fleur isn't just teaching surgeons how to sew; she's showing them how to look. By spending so much time with surgical teams, she's noticed things that the surgeons themselves are unaware of. Her artist's eye registers the colour, texture and consistency of the organs she sees. She notices how team members develop awareness of one another's bodies, coordinating their movements around each other and the patient on the table. She sees how some surgeons have an instinctive sympathy with anatomical planes, organs and structures, separating them without causing damage – and others haven't. She notices how surgeons are able to recognize instantly when something 'isn't right'.

But Fleur doesn't spend all her time with surgeons. Much of her work is with colleagues in the world of textiles, with other lacemakers and embroiderers, and with her students. She wants to talk to them about her surgical projects but she doesn't want to freak them out with talk of blood and guts. In her latest work, she has communicated her insights into medicine through the language she's most fluent in: textiles.

One of Fleur's innovations is her Textile Body. Although it doesn't look anything like a human from the outside, inside its wooden box are layers which are uncannily surgical. Fleur invites people to explore these in the way an operating team would work, separating structures and holding them out of the way with gentleness and care. For the Textile Body, Fleur has chosen textiles that look or feel like human tissues. Vintage lace evokes the skin of an elderly patient. Undoing some buttons reveals knobbly yellow knitting: the abdominal fat. Then come more layers, filmy fabric membranes suggesting the planes of the abdominal cavity. Mysterious structures make you think of nerves and important blood vessels. The idea is not to identify these structures anatomically but to negotiate them without causing damage. The final task is to place a stitch with pinpoint accuracy into a fragile lace structure deep within the Textile Body. To reach it, you must work like a surgeon, separating layers with delicacy and precision. Just as in real surgery, you can't bring that structure to the surface where it's convenient to work on. You have to go to it.

Working on the Textile Body requires surgical skills and surgical sensitivities, but no surgical knowledge. By bringing surgery and textiles together, Fleur has merged two conceptual frameworks, two ways of looking at the world. She has combined the thinking of art and medicine to create something nobody has thought of before. She has broken through the boundaries of her field and taken it in a new direction.

Fleur wouldn't have been able to do that if she hadn't spent years becoming an expert herself. Yet just going through those stages wouldn't have been enough. In order to make her conceptual leap, Fleur needed the opportunity to move outside her field and the insight to imagine how these worlds could be connected.

Ripples on the pond

The Thread Management event in 2014 was like throwing a stone into a pond and watching the ripples. Though many of the participants were medical, the focus wasn't medicine – it was threads. Because the Art Workers' Guild is not a clinical setting, surgical suturing became just one instance of expert threadwork.

Many people in that room were much more skilled with threads than me. They had a wider awareness, experience and understanding of how threads behave. That's only natural, since handling threads is a small part of a surgeon's work but a major one for textile artists or puppeteers. And once the focal point was redefined, traditional hierarchies no longer held. We were not discussing whether operating on sick children was more or less 'important' than fishing or puppetry. Like John Wickham and his team of innovators, everyone contributed something different, yet of equal value.

You have to become an expert before you can change direction like Fleur, John Wickham and Will. There are no shortcuts here. You have to go through those years of hard graft and cope with the ups and downs that make you the expert you've become. You have to earn your spurs. But once you've experienced this process from the inside, you have the skills you need to bring about change. Then it's a question of imagination, of stepping back from the *how* of being expert to the *why*; to the meaning and purpose of your work. It makes you question what being an expert means, why it matters to you and how you can pass your knowledge on. That's what the next chapter is about.

11. Passing it on

I'm teaching a group of GPs how to do simple surgical procedures, and I'm having a problem with Michael. It's the early 1990s, I've recently changed from surgery to general practice, and I'm running the first of a series of educational courses. Michael is an experienced GP, but he just doesn't seem to get what I'm showing him. I'm explaining how to hold instruments and tie knots. He seems clumsy, and I can't understand why he can't do what I ask. It's not as if I'm trying to teach him anything complicated – just obvious things that any doctor should know.

Soon after I joined my partnership I started teaching family doctors to carry out 'minor surgery'. At that time, GPs were being encouraged by the government to do this kind of work. Most of it involved seemingly straightforward procedures, like excising lumps and bumps under local anaesthetic. But often the GPs had little or no surgical experience, so not surprisingly things didn't always go well. Sometimes they didn't send the lumps they removed for laboratory analysis, and skin cancers were missed. Sometimes they made large incisions and struggled to close them, resulting in unsightly scars. Sometimes they chose an inappropriate treatment altogether.

Because of my surgical experience, I was invited to develop a training programme for the UK, funded by the government and supported by the Royal Colleges of Surgeons and General Practitioners. Working with the simulation company Limbs & Things, we developed latex models of those lumps and bumps, so the GPs could practise procedures without damaging real people. I also designed a three-day course and took it to centres around the UK.

Like Michael, many of the doctors on those courses really struggled. Though most of them knew far more than I did about general practice, they couldn't seem to do the simplest things with their hands. They used the wrong instrument to hold a suture needle. They struggled to tie a secure knot in a piece of thread. They couldn't use dissecting forceps without causing damage. At first I couldn't understand it. I knew that it wasn't because they were clumsy or stupid or uninterested – far from it.

Then I realized that it was because nobody had ever taught them these apparently straightforward skills. The surgeons they had watched as medical students or junior doctors were so expert they made everything look easy. It dawned on me that there was a kind of knowledge that experts assumed everyone had, but non-experts didn't know existed. Michael wasn't grappling with something simple at all. It only seemed simple to me because I knew how to do it. To him it wasn't like that. There was a huge gap between my understanding and his.

Crossing the ha-ha

I'll use a metaphor from landscape gardening to illustrate the gap that can stretch between teacher and student. In many eighteenth-century country estates, the large house and garden are set in extensive parkland stocked with animals. The curiously named 'ha-ha' is a deep ditch between the garden and the surrounding park. Cattle and deer appear to come right up to the flowerbeds, creating an illusion that the house is in the midst of untamed nature. But the animals never eat the flowers – because they can't reach them. Viewed from the park, the sheer, brick-faced vertical wall of the ditch is obvious and unscalable. But viewed from the house, the ha-ha is invisible.

As experts, we are in the house, viewing an unbroken landscape that stretches across the park. When we see a novice some distance away, there seems no reason why they should not just walk a bit further and join us. But the novice is in the park, and from there the gulf to the house is impassable. When I was teaching Michael how to tie a surgical knot, he was in the park and I was in the house.

At this point on the path to becoming expert, you've made the transition from Journeyman to Master. You have passed through all the stages and reached the top of your field. You've become an expert, and now you want to pass on the knowledge you've gained. But it's often much more difficult than you expect. You have to make another transition, this time from doing things yourself to helping other people do them. This is something all teachers grapple with. In my case the subject was surgical techniques, but it's the same when it's a new computer program, a sport or a language. How can you bridge that ha-ha?

Thinking about Michael, help came from an unlikely quarter – the world of music. One day, between those minor surgery courses, I was having a harpsichord lesson with Sophie Yates. I've been learning with Sophie for over twenty years and she's an expert in every sense. She's a distinguished performer who gives concerts all over the world. She's a recording artist with a long list of credits. She often appears on the radio to discuss her passion for early music. And she's an expert teacher.

On this occasion, I was grappling with ornaments in a suite by François Couperin, the French baroque composer. Couperin's writing is all about detail and precision, about the placing of trills and the spacing of notes. Sophie's teaching, too, is all about detail – not vague instructions to 'make it more expressive' or 'loosen the rhythm', but specifics I can work with. She shows me tiny changes to timing, touch and finger position that make all the difference.

At the keyboard, I played the passage I'd been struggling with. Sophie listened, then asked me to play the first few bars again. She could tell what the problem was, but I couldn't, so she tried several approaches. She described what she wanted to hear, but I couldn't grasp what she meant. Then she demonstrated by playing the bar herself – now I could see her point and hear the difference, but I still couldn't do it myself. After trying a few approaches without success, Sophie put her hand over mine, made a minute adjustment to the angle of my wrist and suddenly things fell into place – a physical solution that couldn't be put into words.

Sophie had found a way to unlock my difficulty, to identify my problem and help me fix it. To me, this is the essence of 'passing it on'. Passing it on is a conversation, a dialogue; not a one-way process. Sophie was building on her decades of experience to pinpoint what was relevant to me at that moment. She had to know how to play that passage herself, of course, but also how to convey it to me, how to find a point of connection. It wasn't about her demonstrating something she could do and I couldn't. That wouldn't help me learn. It was about me, her pupil, stuck at an earlier stage along the path. I realized that what I was trying to do as a teacher with the GPs was what Sophie was doing with me as a pupil. Sophie and I had both become experts in our fields, and now we were finding ways of passing it on.

For a long time, I'd seen music as an antidote to work, and it never occurred to me that there might be similarities between learning music and learning surgery. Yet if *how* you learn, rather than *what* you learn, becomes the focus, these examples become instances of the same thing – an expert teacher finding ways to help a learner to understand and to do. This communication cannot happen through books alone, or even through images. It takes place at the intersection between your body, another person's body and the physical world around you both. An expert teacher reveals unsayable things by demonstrating, and by highlighting whatever is crucial for you at that moment. A teacher must identify the problem which they and their student are trying to address.

I tried to work out Sophie's secret. Of course, she's gone through the same process as all the experts in this book. She's done her time, carried out her share of boring repetitive work. She's spent years practising scales, learning music theory, perfecting her performance technique, mastering repertoire and researching the history of her field.

In her teaching, Sophie starts by identifying one thing her student finds difficult, and working on that. Her ability to nail the problem is uncanny. Sometimes it's to do with understanding the structure of the music. Sometimes it's a technical issue, like a tiny change to the angle of one hand, a detail of fingering, or even just sitting closer to the keyboard. Sometimes it's something wider, such as needing to choose a different piece of music altogether.

Above all, Sophie listens. Then she translates her listening into action. In our lessons, she notices what I'm playing in a way that I can't, because I'm too close. She registers the details of articulation and phrasing which I miss, because I'm struggling with the mechanics of performance. My focus is on pressing the right keys in the right order at the right time. But Sophie doesn't only hear the notes I play. She notices the spaces between, the places where the music needs to breathe. She pinpoints what I'm grappling with and puts her finger on problems I haven't spotted. Her expert ears hear things I'm not aware of.

Dealing with technical issues is Sophie's starting point with me, because that's what I've framed as my problem and that's where I think I need help. But Sophie has a wider picture in her sights. She notices things that go beyond technical difficulty – things about my confidence and my approach to practice and performance. She guides me across terrain she has travelled but which I haven't yet encountered. I know that she has spent years in the stages I've described in this book, and now she's using that experience to help me.

Alan Spivey, one of my colleagues at Imperial, is professor of synthetic chemistry. He does something similar with the students on his course. They spend a lot of time learning facts and theories. They also learn laboratory skills and techniques by attending 'practicals'. They have to be meticulous, noticing and documenting what they do in minute detail. Tiny changes can be the difference between success and failure when you're developing a new reaction. But technical accuracy is only part of the picture. As the students become more experienced, they design and carry out their own experiments to create and test novel compounds.

For Alan, being a synthetic chemist is about connecting practical work with an understanding of molecular structure and reactivity. He can zoom in on these structural details, then zoom out to their implications for experimental design. Not everyone can do this. Alan says his students don't always integrate their work in the lab with their theoretical knowledge. He tries to get them to think in the way he does – to think 'like a chemist' as they move towards becoming research scientists themselves. It's a long process, and not all students get there. Many get stuck along the way.

Getting unstuck

'Threshold concepts' are a useful way to think about this process. According to this theory, learning is not smooth but moves through stages, each a threshold to a deeper understanding. It requires a periodic reframing of your existing knowledge and culminates in thinking *like* an expert musician, scientist, doctor or craftsman, not just doing the things they do. But before that, there is a time when you struggle with 'troublesome knowledge' – the sort of information that you might understand piecemeal, but can't put together into a coherent whole. Sometimes you might find yourself in a 'stuck place'.

Some people can stay in a stuck place almost indefinitely. That's what had happened to my family doctor when I was starting out at medical school, who could never remember the names of all those little buggers in the neck. It's what happened to me when I tried to juggle with five balls, as I described in Chapter 3. Both of us knew what we were trying to do. With juggling, I understood the physics; I knew where my hands were meant to be. But I hadn't mastered the doing. I'm still in that stuck place now, where I understand the elements but they haven't come together. I believe it's far more common than we realize, because people can perform at a high level without full comprehension. Being unable to remember the little buggers in the neck didn't undermine my doctor's ability to care for his patients, but it was a blind spot he had to work around. It's in circumstances like these, when a pupil already has some competence but can't slot things together, that a teacher is invaluable.

For Adrian, juggling with five balls was as easy as three balls eventually became for me. But for some reason I couldn't make the transition he'd made. Partly, this was my own fault. I didn't put in the time that would allow me to coordinate my body. However, Adrian might never have experienced that stuck place himself, and was therefore unable to identify my troublesome knowledge and help me past it. This was what I had found with Michael on the GP minor surgery course. I couldn't understand why he couldn't do what I was showing him, so I couldn't formulate a solution.

Jan Meyer and Ray Land, who developed the idea of threshold concepts, talk about the difficulty of integrating elements which don't yet hang together. Once you cross a threshold and move forward, things fall into place and you experience a different way of knowing – until you reach the next threshold. To do this you need help, and that's where teachers come in. Interestingly, the discomfort of coming to a new way of knowing rapidly disappears after you cross a threshold. That's why some teachers don't seem to understand why their students find things so difficult. The teachers are no longer struggling with what their students are struggling with.

Now that Joshua the tailor has become an expert, he can look back at his teachers and see what worked and what didn't – and then apply that experience to his interactions with his own apprentices. Ron the making tailor, Joshua's first master, was technically excellent but not a skilled teacher. He insisted on mimicry, making Joshua copy exactly what he did without explaining why. Ron had little tolerance for questioning, and took it as a personal affront if Joshua asked him why he did things in a particular way. He was critical without offering support. Though criticality is important, Ron's unwillingness to unpack his reasons meant that Joshua spent a lot of time not knowing what he was doing wrong.

Joshua's second master was Arthur, the cutting tailor. Arthur was completely different. He had a curious mind, and he wanted Joshua to develop one too. Generous with his time, he taught Joshua the foundations of his craft, allowing him to become free and independent. Arthur believed in graduated responsibility, and he only criticized when he thought it would help. Most of the time, he pointed out the positive aspects of Joshua's work. When he did give negative criticism, Joshua knew it was deserved. Above all, Arthur taught Joshua the principles of design and construction, and gave him the confidence to spread his wings.

Sharing your expertise with people less experienced than you is another shift from you to them, though this time the 'them' refers to learners rather than audiences, customers or patients. Sometimes it's about teaching techniques or procedures, and tackling difficulties that block progress. Sometimes it's about encouraging learners to persevere during those dark times we all encounter along the way. Sometimes it's about helping them cope with the unexpected, recover from mistakes, build self-confidence or decide on a career path. This ability to teach, to coach and to inspire is easy to recognize but hard to define.

Back in my minor surgery courses, I struggled to explain to the GPs what I knew but couldn't seem to put into words. I tried giving lectures, where I described instruments and techniques in words. But that didn't work. Even a demonstration didn't solve the problem. With people like Michael, it was only in the practical sessions that things fell into place. There, I could see what each person was having difficulty with, and figure out how to help. I tried different ways of telling and showing. Often it took a few attempts before I hit upon something that worked.

Many of these doctors had chosen a career in general practice because they hadn't enjoyed surgery as a student or a junior doctor. Perhaps because of this, the surgeons they did work for hadn't ensured their learners understood the basics of operative surgery. Those more senior doctors had already crossed a ha-ha and no longer remembered how confusing an array of surgical instruments – such as needle-holders and artery forceps – can be. These instruments look similar, but they work completely differently. If you pick up a suture needle with artery forceps, the needle swivels round in parallel grooves in the instrument's jaws and you can't get a firm grip or place an accurate stitch. If you pick up a bleeding artery with a needle-holder, you crush the tissue and cause serious damage. Nobody tells you that. They just assume you know. But how can you, if you've never been shown?

In my minor surgery courses, I hadn't been able to convey the knowledge those learners needed. As a result, both they and I started to feel frustrated. Then I tried Sophie's approach. When I saw someone struggling to tie a knot or control a needle, I'd put my hand over theirs and show them how a tiny shift in the angle of their wrist could make all the difference. Once they felt it, things started to make sense.

'Two Zebras Buggered My Cat'

Having gone through the stages of becoming an expert doesn't mean you can remember what it was like at the time. Being an expert yourself doesn't necessarily mean you can teach other people. You can't pass on your experience to someone else before they've completed at least some of the steps themselves. And it takes insight, imagination, empathy and humility to put yourself back on the other side of the ha-ha.

I experienced this at the start of my career when I became an anatomy demonstrator at the University of Manchester, where I'd been a medical student. Nobody explained the teaching part of being a demonstrator, so I had to learn on the job. By that time I'd qualified as a doctor and had spent a year in a hospital as a houseman, working flat out to look after the patients on my ward. The prospect of teaching anatomy came as a welcome change. For one thing, I wouldn't be looking after patients, which meant a whole year without being on call. No more getting bleeped throughout the night to re-site drips and unblock catheters.

But demonstrating anatomy was a steep learning curve. The academics in the department assumed I'd 'just know' how to teach. But I didn't. Every week I'd take four different groups through the same part of the body. Each group of ten students had their own cadaver, and they would spend the morning or afternoon dissecting.

Though my own focus was on the surgical exams I was preparing for, I knew that my main role in the department was to teach those first-year undergraduates. Much of what I was going to be tested on in my surgical exams wasn't relevant to them and I had to avoid cluttering up their minds with excessive detail. My job was to 'demonstrate', to show them what they would need to know as doctors, to be a guide.

Becoming a guide wasn't just about conveying anatomical knowledge or the techniques of dissection. It was about understanding what the students were struggling with. In the process, I developed my voice as a teacher of anatomy. I tried to put myself back in their position. That wasn't too difficult, as I was only one step ahead of them with my anatomical knowledge. So I shared things I'd found helpful, like the colourful mnemonics I'd learned when I was a student. Some of these have stayed with me ever since, like a burr in a hiking sock. Although I'd struggle now to remember the five terminal branches of the facial nerve in isolation (temporal, zygomatic, buccal, marginal mandibular, cervical), *Two Zebras Buggered My Cat* has never left me.

I found that one of the biggest challenges as a teacher is deciding what *not* to point out. It's easy to swamp a learner with long lists, but less is often more. The art of teaching is to find one or two things which need to be improved upon – and which the learner can do something about – then leave the rest for another day. That's what Sophie does in her harpsichord lessons. She doesn't focus on obvious things like fumbled scale passages or wrong notes, because she knows they can be fixed later. Instead, she points out things I haven't noticed.

That's what Arthur the cutting tailor was teaching Joshua too. He wasn't concerned about small-scale glitches, or things that could be easily remedied. His focus was on Joshua's grasp of tailoring principles.

Each of these experienced teachers homed in on a single thing at a time that could be done better. Each of them did it in a way that helped their student move forward and build their confidence. Each of them was demonstrating care.

Much later, I became familiar with the work of Lev Vygotsky, the Soviet psychologist whose theories have had a profound impact on my own approach to learning. Vygotsky died in 1934, and for decades his work remained relatively unknown in the West, but over the years his ideas about social constructivism have become increasingly influential. One of his concepts is the 'zone of proximal development' or ZPD. The idea here is that any learner comes with things they can already do. At the same time, there are whole areas that are completely out of reach. In between are things they can achieve with expert help but cannot do on their own. That's the ZPD. Here the role of a teacher is pivotal, giving people support when they need it, and having the sensitivity to back off when they are no longer required. Nobody wants someone breathing down their neck while they are practising something they're getting the hang of but which just needs more work. A skilful teacher provides temporary scaffolding, like a skyscraper under construction. As soon as the building is strong enough to take its own weight, the scaffolding can be dismantled.

Sophie was working with me in my ZPD when she was adjusting the position of my hand at the keyboard; she gave me a new insight which I could work on by myself. I was joining my students in their ZPD when I was an anatomy demonstrator, and again when teaching GPs to do minor surgery. Clive, my wise tutor, did something similar when the other doctors and I were watching one another's video consultations in Chapter 8. Whatever your area of work, having someone who can support you in your own ZPD is essential. And becoming skilled in recognizing the boundaries of a learner's ZPD is part of passing it on.

When Arthur the cutting tailor was nearing retirement, he encouraged Joshua to take on more responsibility. One day, he said, 'The next new customer who comes in, you can have.' After an initial meeting with this new customer, Joshua arranged an appointment for the next fitting. But then the man came in to explain that he needed his suit to be made very quickly, for an important family occasion. At that point, Joshua expected Arthur to take over. But he didn't. Instead, he said, 'Well, you'll have to work fast then, won't you,' and left Joshua to get on with it. By gauging the extent of Joshua's ZPD, Arthur gave him the confidence he needed to work under pressure. Arthur was able to let go.

As a teacher, you can't be in control forever. At a certain point you have to hand over; constantly standing over someone doesn't help. You can't keep telling people how to do things, and you can't force them to do things your way. You have to allow your students or the people in your team to get things wrong, to take responsibility for their mistakes. That's how they'll learn. Passing it on requires you to be there when you're needed, and to fade into the background when you're not.

Maps and guides

So what does 'passing it on' entail? What is this final step on the journey to becoming expert, when you become a Master and take responsibility for the learning of others? To me, it's a combination of being a guide, a mentor and a coach. To explain this, I'll use the metaphor of a map.

Throughout your progression towards becoming expert, you need help in finding the way. In the early stages of doing time you need instruction in specific tasks. That's how things work when you're an Apprentice. This is like using the satnav on your mobile phone when you're delivering a parcel in a city. You have to get from where you are to where you're going, and the system tells you how to do that. It doesn't ask you to think, but expects you to follow its directions. A voice in your ear says, 'In two hundred yards, turn left.' If you follow the instructions closely enough, you will almost certainly get to the right place. But you'll have no idea of how your route fits into the wider landscape. At this point, that doesn't matter – provided you do what you're told, you'll have done what's expected of you.

When Joshua was making pocket flaps, when Fabrice was sweeping hair from the salon floor and when I was doing the bloods, we were all following instructions. We were all using our satnav. Nobody was interested in whether we grasped the bigger picture. They just wanted us to do the tasks they had given us. Our masters would check that we were doing the tasks they specified, but that was all.

Later, as you start to understand more about the work, satnav instructions aren't enough. You need a map. You're developing a sense of where to go, and you realize there are different ways to get there. With a physical journey, you might start with a road atlas that marks out routes schematically. That helps you pick a route as you go from one part of the country to another. These are the sort of maps I encountered as a medical student, setting out the canon I needed to memorize and refer to. But that detailed information about anatomy, physiology, diseases and their treatments seemed out of context at first, unrelated to anything I'd encountered in real life. It was the same with Joshua, whose pocket flaps didn't make much sense until they became part of a jacket.

At first it seemed a morass of information and I couldn't pick out what was important from what wasn't. That's where lecturers, tutors and anatomy demonstrators come in. You need help to check that your route makes sense.

Once you set out, it's helpful to see the terrain in more detail. You move from a road atlas to an Ordnance Survey (OS) map. OS maps show hills, rivers, buildings and fields, as well as roads and footpaths. But although you can plan where you're going, even an OS map doesn't tell you what you'll find when you get there. You'll be dealing with all kinds of things that aren't on the map at all – recent buildings, or changes to stiles and fences. You'll grapple with bad weather, getting lost, becoming tired, and all the other challenges of a cross-country trip. And you'll have to interpret all that as you go, integrating the knowledge from the map with what you find when you get there.

People who make maps are not always the ones who use them, and they don't always give you the information you need. An experienced walker who knows a region well needs much less in the way of contextual detail than a newcomer to the area. That leads to those infuriating sketches that only make sense if you're in the head of the person who has drawn them. If you miss a gate or a stile or take a wrong turning, you're off the map, without the information you need in order to recognize where you are and get back on track.

Guidebooks or instruction manuals can be useful here, but people writing guidebooks often make assumptions about what a reader will know. I read one recently that said 'cross the next field, heading towards a piebald horse under a beech tree'. The author must have lapsed into an assumption that the landscape he saw that day was fixed and static.

Thinking that other people will know what is in your mind is a mistake that's surprisingly easy to make. It's like those teachers who get exasperated because a learner doesn't seem able to grasp the point. In fact, it is the responsibility of the teacher to recognize and adjust to the level of knowledge and understanding a learner comes with, rather than starting with what the teacher wants to teach. Here, you need more than a map or a guidebook. You need a human guide.

As you move along your path you'll often find that your maps don't work. When I became a GP, most of mine turned out to be useless. As a surgeon, I'd spent years treating patients who had been sorted by someone else and whose problems had been defined as 'surgical'. Suddenly, as a GP, I was the first port of call. Not only did I have to remember things I'd learned at medical school a decade earlier and promptly forgotten, but I had to find my way in a new landscape.

Sometimes my patients would have a serious condition that needed immediate action. Then I felt on firm ground. More often, though, they had common, self-limiting problems that weren't particularly serious and would settle down on their own. At first it was difficult to tell the difference, and often I overreacted. I mistook straightforward things I hadn't encountered before for problems that needed referral. But a lot of the time I couldn't pigeonhole my patients at all. They'd say things like, 'I don't know what it is, Doctor, but I just don't feel right', or the classic 'I feel tired all the time'. I didn't know what the problem was, and neither did they. I struggled to distinguish between diagnostic signal and noise. The maps I'd come with didn't make sense. I needed a guide.

A guide has travelled the route you're on and knows what to expect. They can tell you if you're drifting off the path, and show you how to get back. As a surgeon, my guides were the consultants I worked for, the doctors in my community of practice, and the nurses and other professionals who helped me learn. But although a guide has responsibility for making sure you reach where you've said you want to go, that's where their responsibility ends. Provided you get to your destination safely, their job is over. Deciding what to do when you get there, or where to go next, is not their concern. For that, you need more than a guide. You need a mentor, perhaps even a coach.

So far I've talked about journeys as if the destination is already decided. But as you become independent, moving from Apprentice to Journeyman to Master, you have to make a lot of decisions. As well as moving 'from you to them' and developing your voice, you have to choose where to go. It's here that you need someone who cares for you as a person. A mentor does exactly that.

That's what I was fortunate to have when I became a

GP trainee, and again with Clive, my trainer. That's what Joshua experienced with Arthur, his inspirational cutting tailor. That's what I hear from all the experts I've met. Passing it on goes far beyond providing training in techniques or procedures. Passing it on means nurturing and supporting someone as they move along a path that you yourself have followed.

But maps are never neutral. They present what the map-maker wants to show you, which isn't necessarily what you need to know. A good mentor will teach you to be sceptical about maps and to use your judgement in interpreting them. In his 1977 book *A Guide for the Perplexed*, the economist E. F. Schumacher describes his experience with maps during the time of the Cold War:

> On a visit to Leningrad some years ago, I consulted a map to find out where I was, but I could not make it out. From where I stood, I could see several enormous churches, yet there was no trace of them on my map. When finally an interpreter came to help me, he said: 'We don't show churches on our maps.' Contradicting him, I pointed to one that was very clearly marked. 'That is a museum,' he said, 'not what we call a "living church". It is only the "living churches" that we don't show.'
>
> It then occurred to me that this was not the first time I had been given a map that failed to show many things I could see right in front of my eyes. All through

school and university I had been given maps of life and knowledge on which there was hardly a trace of many of the things that I most cared about and that seemed to me to be of the greatest possible importance for the conduct of my life. I remembered that for many years my perplexity had been complete; and no interpreter had come along to help me. It remained complete until I ceased to suspect the sanity of my perceptions and began, instead, to suspect the soundness of the maps.

Going off-piste

Back with Michael on the minor surgery course, he suddenly sees what I'm getting at. He moves his hand a fraction, and something falls into place. Now he can tie that knot, get that suture tension just right. But he's still finding it more difficult than I expected. During a coffee break I ask him what he thinks the problem is.

He tells me that ever since childhood he's struggled with being clumsy, but he thought it was just how he was. It's only recently that he's had some tests which show he's got mild dyspraxia, a developmental disorder of coordination. It never occurred to me that there might be an underlying physical reason for Michael's problems with handling instruments and tying knots. I realize that passing it on isn't just about telling people things you know, or showing them things you can do.

It's about putting yourself in their position and walking beside them on *their* path to becoming expert. Passing it on is not about me as a teacher, but about Michael and what he needs.

In the final chapter, I'll ask why experts matter to all of us.

APPRENTICE | JOURNEYMAN | MASTER

PASSING
IT ON

'IT'S NOT
ABOUT YOU'

DOING
TIME

USING YOUR
SENSES

DEVELOPING
VOICE

SPACE AND
OTHER PEOPLE

12. Why experts matter

When I noticed damp in my house, I called Richard, an expert recommended by a friend. Richard listened as I described the problem, then walked around my basement and peered at the walls and the floor. He got out a meter and took some readings. After collecting his thoughts, he outlined what he saw as the issue, suggested some possible approaches, and recommended the option he thought best. Rather to my surprise, it turned out to be one of the less expensive ones.

I asked Richard how he'd decided what to advise. He explained that he'd been in the business for almost forty years, and had worked in a lot of houses like mine. He'd seen similar problems many times and tried all kinds of solutions. Although some new materials and technologies had recently become available, he felt that a conservative approach would work best in my case. He believed that what he suggested would fix the problem, though he didn't know for certain. If it didn't, there were other avenues we could explore. We agreed to go ahead on that basis.

At that point, I had no direct evidence of Richard's technical skills, though my friend had said they were excellent. My relationship was with Richard as a person – as an expert in his field. Richard had started by identifying my problem. He wasn't thinking only of meter readings, and he wasn't out for a short-term profit. Instead, he used his experience to suggest a way forward that made sense to us both. I trusted him and what he said, because I believed he was an expert. Richard did what I do as a clinician, what Joshua does as a tailor, and what the other experts in this book are so good at.

What the experts say

We all need experts like Richard because we rely on what they do; when we have problems, we need experts to fix them. When we are ill, we need doctors. When we fly, we need pilots. When we have a problem in our basement, we need specialists in treating damp. Yet the talk today about experts often leaves me angry. In this final chapter, I'll explain why.

I often hear experts dismissed as irrelevant – no longer of value in a rapidly changing world. I hear them written off as a useless elite. Yet nothing could be further from the truth, as we all realize when we are sick, or on an aeroplane, or find damp in our house.

But the services which experts provide are only part of their importance. *Becoming* expert is at the core of being human. It doesn't matter if we end up *as* an expert, recognized by our peers and the wider world – what matters is that we become better at whatever we strive to achieve. Whatever our interests, devoting years to something worthwhile meets a deep need: to immerse ourselves in something bigger than we are.

In this book, I've tracked the internal processes of becoming expert. These processes are less often written about than the declarative knowledge or component skills of 'expertise'. Partly that's because knowledge and skill are easier to demonstrate and test. But it's also because, as an insider, it's easy to lose sight of the stages you went through as you became expert. Soon that experience of *becoming* disappears from view, however tough you found it at the time. But it's that very experience that's so important and so worthwhile. Becoming expert is about channelling our energies into something that has purpose and meaning. It's about making use of the potential we all have, to achieve something that goes beyond humdrum everyday life.

Becoming an expert of this kind involves a shift in who you are, not just in how much you know and what you can do. In this book, I distinguish between the knowing that focuses on process – the skills and procedural knowledge of a plumber, a tailor or a surgeon – and the transformations that go on underneath. Becoming expert is about your relationship with your work and the people you do it for and with. It allows you to work with thin materials on the verge of collapse, to judge when to act and when to hold back, to let someone else go ahead and make mistakes because you know they have to learn.

I believe that we all have the capacity to become expert, whether we recognize it or not. Of course, not everyone can become an international concert pianist, a surgical pioneer, a famous sculptor or a Nobel Prize–winning scientist. Most people wouldn't want to – becoming a Nobel Prize–winning scientist is to live your whole life for science. But we're all on a path, we all do things we care about, and we can all get better at doing them. The ideas in this book will resonate with anyone who joins a basketball club, gives presentations to colleagues at work, learns a foreign language, goes to a pottery class or designs spreadsheets. Becoming expert is about recognizing our potential and letting it grow. Like a deep ocean current, becoming expert may not be visible on the surface, but its effects are profound.

While it's clear that we need experts, we often think of them as a species apart. We overlook the fact that we can all become expert ourselves, or at least move in that direction. Though the taxidermists, tailors and magicians in this book might seem exotic, we can all aspire to do what they do, though to a different extent and in our own area of interest. But we often fail to see the parallels between what such experts have gone through and what we are experiencing ourselves. We don't recognize them as examples of what we can become.

All the experts in this book have something in common: what they do is central to who they are. This doesn't mean that becoming expert is restricted to your main occupation. Your passion may be dismissively described by others as a 'hobby'. But many people are more expert at their hobby than their 'proper' job.

Becoming expert does not depend on how society gauges the value of your work, for society is fickle and inconstant. And it's not about fame or money either. Instead, it's about the path you take. If you are going through the stages in this book, as I believe we all are, you are on your way to becoming expert, whether you're a plumber, a pilot or a Sunday painter.

I've tried to give a realistic sense of what this path is like. It's not a steady climb upwards; it's more like a difficult mountain pass. You might have to descend to get around some obstacle before you can continue. You'll go through bleak times when you feel you're standing still or going backwards. It takes belief and perseverance to stick with it, to realize that the path is going upwards overall. Becoming expert takes time – lots of time.

I hope this book has helped to counter the argument that you can do everything in a rush. I am aware that there are courses on the internet that claim to teach you to speak a language, play a musical instrument or become an investment banker in just one month. But these short, snipped-up experiences aren't satisfying alternatives to a long-term commitment. You can't master the guitar in a month, because there isn't an end point to mastering the guitar. You can start, but you never finish. That's the fascination of becoming expert.

Even in a fast-moving society like ours, some things remain constant. We need experts to move us around the world, treat us when we're sick, fix things when they go wrong, create beauty and inspire us. The specifics do change, of course. Things that were taken for granted become obsolete. For the most part we no longer develop photographs in darkrooms, use manual typewriters or send telegrams, so we no longer need experts in those areas. Now we have different approaches to creating images, communicating at distance and writing text. Soon, these too will change. Yet the developments of the future will require experts as much as the past ever did – more so, as the complexity of our world increases. Robotics, artificial intelligence, new forms of energy, the responsible stewardship of resources – all these will depend on experts. And those experts of the future must apply themselves to their craft with the same sense of purpose as Derek the taxidermist, Andrew the wood engraver and Joshua the tailor do today. Although their fields may be very different, the process will remain the same.

Toxins and nutrients

The opportunity to become expert should be one of our inalienable rights. It's how we fulfil our potential as human beings. Yet the slow process required is at odds with demands for instant gratification. There's a growing sense that anyone can learn to do anything – and quickly. But that's not the case. Becoming expert involves sticking at something for much longer than you normally would. Of course, just persevering doesn't automatically turn you into an expert, and there are plenty of people who keep doing the same thing and don't get much better – like me with my juggling.

Like any organic process, becoming expert needs nutrients. These include guidance and encouragement, exposure to mistakes, opportunities for spending time with your materials and the people you work with, and allowing your personality to unfold. I've described this path as if you started when you become an Apprentice. I've told the stories of people in specialized fields where it can seem that their careers only began when they joined their workshop, studio or salon. But there is always a background. Throughout our childhood we are immersed in a world of the senses, experiencing the world and the people around us. At home and at school, we stock our internal library of sensations, knowledge and skills which we build on later. We need to experience what it is to look, hear, touch, sniff and taste; to work with other people; to share space and to negotiate our wishes around theirs. Becoming expert is part of a story which begins when we are born.

Yet in many parts of the world, including the United Kingdom, conditions for becoming expert are under threat. These threats include a relentless pressure to speed everything up, a narrowing of school curriculums, and a neoliberal mindset that sees everything in terms of the bottom line and places short-term profit over long-term value. More pressure comes from reduced social contact and dwindling opportunities for engaging physically with the material world. Paradoxically, as we are becoming more connected globally, local isolation is getting worse. Opportunities for shared doing are becoming scarcer.

Concentration and focus are being nibbled away at by the demands of email and social media. The urgent takes precedence over the important, and pressures for an immediate response can be overwhelming. Gradual processes are under attack, whether in food, reading or craftsmanship. Slow learning is being squeezed by political pressure to achieve qualifications faster, with less effort and fewer resources. Qualifications themselves are skewed by an obsession with assessment. But quantifying what students learn at the expense of how they learn it is dangerously short-sighted.

Young people are being deprived of the opportunities they need to make the most of their potential. When newcomers start in an expert field, we expect them to have basic skills of reading, writing, arithmetic and using a computer, to have an understanding of the world around them. We expect a basic fluency in the physical world, an understanding that is built through years of exposure at home and at school. We expect people to relate to others they work alongside, to behave responsibly and to look out for one another's safety. If we can no longer take that fluency for granted, we must do something to redress it, or make allowances for the time it will take to build up later. We know the conditions that becoming expert requires, yet we are allowing them to be destroyed.

I've noticed this at the university where I work. Until recently, you could assume that first-year students would arrive with a range of basic skills they'd learned at home and school through working with their hands. Cutting with scissors and paper, sticking things together with glue, writing with a pen, tying knots in shoelaces and string – all skills which should develop throughout childhood. Some people are more dextrous or confident than others, of course, but there was a baseline you could rely on, a shared experience of having done stuff. Young people had also learned to do things in front of others, through music, drama and dance. Even if they weren't good performers in a conventional sense, they had gained vital experience.

In recent years, my colleagues and I have found that we can no longer make these assumptions. Young people entering science and medicine at our university have excellent academic results, but many struggle to tie a firm knot, cut out a shape with scissors, or speak in front of other people. Though a glance at the UK state secondary school curriculum gives a clue as to why this is, my students come from all over the world, which makes me think the problem is global.

Art, design, music, dance, cooking and other subjects that involve dexterity and performance are being eradicated from the curriculum. Even science subjects are taught in an abstracted way, with few opportunities to work in a laboratory and carry out experiments for yourself. Pupils in science lessons have their chemicals measured out for them in advance, to save teachers' time and make sure that the practicals 'work'. Opportunities for error are being eliminated by an institutional aversion to risk. Young people no longer experience what it feels like to get things wrong and have to put them right.

There is also a pernicious tendency to divide and categorize our lives. 'Doing' is relegated to the art room, yet art rooms are being abolished. Performance is confined to music or drama, yet music and drama are being cut out. This is a tragedy and a disgrace. We are stripping people of their birthright – their confidence to work with the material world around them. Talking to a head teacher at a north London school, I was horrified to learn that some pupils are unable to hold a pen or use a pair of scissors because they have never had the opportunity to try. This is not for lack of will on the part of the school. Quite the opposite. It comes from a combination of decades of inadequate resourcing and a lack of insight into how people become expert. This is not just a problem for young people coming into the system now. It's a problem for us all.

The push for quick results is having an especially baneful effect. A preoccupation with visual, screen-based information is making the problem more evident. Young people learn about chemistry experiments by watching scientists online, not by doing the work themselves. The sounds and smells of science are being sanitized. People are becoming spectators, not participants. Sensory richness is being flattened by technologies which privilege sight over the other senses.

As you'll have seen so far, I'm all in favour of technology. I'm writing this book on a laptop computer. I have worked throughout my career with people who operate at the cutting edge of technological innovation, and I am excited that each new generation will be expert in things that I can't yet conceive of. My point is that we should use technological advances and social change to enrich our experiences, not impoverish them.

We are in a perilous place at the moment. We risk losing skills without even noticing that they're disappearing, like habitat loss elsewhere in the world. The statistics are alarming. In the United Kingdom, school exam entries in creative subjects have fallen by over 20 per cent since 2010, and entries in design and technology have fallen by 57 per cent. The skills of doing are being wrenched out of curriculums. There is an insidious assumption that science is more productive than the arts, and that there is no place for art within science. This is short-sighted to the point of madness.

Myopic initiatives to 'streamline' systems which have evolved over many years are hollowing out the expertise of communities. That mixture of 'newcomers and old-timers', as Lave and Wenger put it, is disappearing. Becoming expert is seen as individual, not collective. Yet all the stories in this book show how much we depend on one another, on communities of practice, as we move along our own path to becoming expert.

This is not a nostalgic yearning for an imaginary golden age. There are plenty of bad things about the old-fashioned apprenticeship system. It encouraged bullying and exploitation. It expected inhuman levels of work. It put a system ahead of those within it. Often, it stultified initiative and prevented people from realizing their potential, keeping them in dead-end roles long after they should have progressed, or not allowing them to participate at all.

It's not all doom and gloom, however. Domains of practice may come and go, but reports of the death of experts have been much exaggerated. Becoming expert remains a basic human need, and the opportunity to pursue that path should be there for every one of us. The threats are real, but they can be countered. The people in this book are living proof of that. They exemplify the principles I've outlined: paying close attention for a long time to something worthwhile that requires and repays sustained commitment; subordinating your desires to the needs of other people; and becoming as good as you can be, even if your area of interest falls outside the mainstream.

As I said earlier, the ecosystem of expertise depends on nutrients which we have a responsibility to deliver. These nutrients include a supportive environment, having basic material needs provided for, and becoming part of a group of like-minded people. A nutrient-rich environment should provide opportunities to gain physical skill, factual knowledge and a sensitivity to materials and people.

Perhaps the biggest threat of all is impatience. We are losing sight of the need for slow learning. Learners need time and support. Experts only emerge through a long process of growth and maturation, like trees growing in a forest. Like trees, experts need to develop without being uprooted and transplanted. Uprooting and trans-planting wastes energy on new rooting that would be far better spent on growing upwards.

When it happens as it should, travelling the path to becoming expert is like a personal relationship. It has the potential to sustain and enrich. It offers great satisfaction and invites lifelong contribution in return. Like other long-term relationships, it doesn't have a clear-cut end. Large enough and flexible enough to contain your growth and evolution, it grows and evolves with you.

The end?

So what is being expert? How do you know when you've become one? The truth is, you never really get there. The path to becoming expert doesn't have an end. So I'll finish with some thoughts about writing this book, using it as a mirror for the ideas it contains.

This is the first book I've written on my own, so I'm not an expert author. Yet it's not the first time I've written anything, so it's a point along my path to becoming expert. That process started at primary school, when I learned the letters of the alphabet and put them together to make simple words. Over the years I've done a lot of writing, from student exams and GP referral letters to essays and scientific papers. But it wasn't until I started writing this book that these stages I've gone through became coherent.

As I was doing time with all that writing, I was using my senses, responding to what other people had written, and sharpening my ideas about what worked and what didn't. I developed a feel for the kind of writer I wanted to become. I got a sense of thin materials on the verge of collapse, of how much I could squeeze a sentence before it lost its meaning or how far I could stretch it before it snapped. I tried things out, got them wrong and had to put them right.

At first my focus was on myself and how I wanted to say things. But then I had to make the transition 'from you to them'. I had to shift from what I wanted to write to what other people would find interesting to read. I had to think how my work would land. I began to develop my voice, my style, my individuality. Now I'm working on how to combine all that to express ideas I've been struggling to articulate for decades, and how to move my field in a different direction.

For each step forward there have been two steps back. I've had to improvise, to respond to the contexts I work in and the people I meet. I've kept reframing my ideas and thinking of new ways to express them. But now I have to stop. I know this book will never be as good as it could be. But sooner or later you need to perform what you've been practising, share it with other people and move on. Echoing Paul Valéry the poet, my editor put it like this: you never finish a book; you just decide when to abandon it.

For me, that sense of never quite being finished lies at the heart of becoming expert. It's an unending process with an elusive goal, but it meets a need in all of us. It's what Andrew Davidson in Chapter 4 meant when he said, 'For more than forty years I've been trying to make the perfect print from a woodblock. I never have, and I know I never will. But I'll never stop trying.' It's what Joshua Byrne meant when he said that he knows there's no such thing as a perfect suit, but he'll always keep trying to make one. It's what I feel about being a doctor, too. There's no perfect operation and no perfect consultation. But we should never stop trying. It's what the path to becoming expert is all about.

Acknowledgements

Expert draws on conversations and collaborations with countless people over several decades. Though I cannot mention all those people by name, my debt to them is incalculable. As anyone who has compiled an invitation list of fairy godmothers will be painfully aware, there is always a danger of forgetting someone who should have been included. If I have done that, I hope I will escape the traditional consequences of such an omission.

In this book, I draw on many experts. They have been extraordinarily generous with their time, their insights and their encouragement, and they have influenced my thinking profoundly. Some appear and reappear throughout my story. Joshua Byrne has shaped my thinking since we first met over ten years ago, and our conversations form the foundation of this book. Fleur Oakes, Richard McDougall, Will Houstoun, Fabrice Ringuet and Sophie Yates have helped me think in new ways about the steps on the path to becoming expert.

Paul Jakeman, Andrew Davidson, Derek Frampton, Duncan Hooson, Phil Bayman, Katharine Coleman, John Launer and Jozef Youssef have all shone light from different perspectives. Andrew Garlick, Alan Spivey, Kirsty Flower, Marta Ajmar, Merlin Strangeway, Liam Noble, Lucy Lyons, David Dolan, Jeremy Jackman, Rachel Warr,

David Owen, Dimitri Bellos, Margot Cooper, Sam Galli-van, Florence Thomas, Harold Ellis, Mary Neiland and Colin Bicknell have helped me develop my ideas.

I have mentioned Thread Management, an event at the Art Workers' Guild. Other events include Thinking with Your Hands and a symposium at Imperial which I called The Art of Performing Science. These, too, have shaped my thinking and provided rich soil for my ideas. Through film and conversation, Paul Craddock has played a central role in all of these events.

A pivotal figure in my thinking has been the semioti-cian and educator Gunther Kress, who died suddenly in June 2019. Our conversations, which took place over more than a decade, were instrumental in developing my ideas for this book. Gunther was a mentor, an inspir-ation and a true friend. I miss him more than I can say.

I have also been inspired by John Wickham, the pion-eering urologist whose work I describe in the book's closing sections. John died in October 2017 at the age of eighty-nine. To me, he captured what being expert is about. Gentle, modest and humane, he too was an inspiration and a friend. His colleagues Mike Kellett, Stuart Greengrass, Chris Russell and Toni Raybould have been immensely helpful, and John's widow Ann has been generosity itself.

Many friends have helped my thinking, especially Julia Anderson. Further back still, my mentors Aylwyn Mannell, Andy Hall and Jeremy Duncan Brown inspired and supported me during my clinical careers. I received unfailing support from my GP partners at Lovemead Group Practice in Trowbridge, Wiltshire – especially Jeremy Bradbrooke and the late Stephen Henry.

I am deeply indebted to the Art Workers' Guild, the extraordinary organization I first mentioned at the start of this book. Many of the experts whose stories I draw on are Brothers (as they are traditionally called, irrespective of gender) of the Guild. As individuals, their insights have been illuminating. As a group, they have made me think in unexpected ways. Being invited to join as a Brother myself has been an honour. Particular thanks must go to Prue Cooper, potter and Past Master of the Guild.

I thank my many colleagues at Imperial College London and beyond, including Fernando Bello, Kirsten Dalrymple and Debra Nestel – long-standing friends and collaborators. I also thank Aaron Williamon of the Royal College of Music – friend, colleague, and joint director with me of the RCM–Imperial Centre for Performance Science.

I thank, too, the staff and students on the Imperial Master in Education (MEd) in Surgical Education and the academics and doctoral students who have helped me develop my ideas. They include Anne Yeh, Sacha Harris, Alex Cope, Tamzin Cuming, Sharon Weldon, Claudia Schlegel and Jeff Bezemer. I thank Barry Smith for his generosity with ideas and insights. And I thank the Wellcome Trust, whose 2012 Engagement Fellowship gave me the freedom to explore the ideas which developed into this book. That opportunity was transformative.

I am indebted to the City and Guilds of London Art School, the Royal Academy of Arts, Gresham College, and many museums and institutions in the UK and overseas for giving me the opportunity to develop my ideas. Also my friend Will Liddell, who first alerted me to the existence of invisible fish.

Next I must thank Jack Ramm, my editor. Jack's contribution has been immense. His commitment, clarity of thought, and support for me as an author – in a word, his care – have been extraordinary. It has been a privilege to work with him. My thanks also to Connor Brown and all the staff at Penguin Books.

Finally, to my family. My daughters Emily and Rachel have been both enthusiastic and encouraging, and with them I have explored many ideas that cross disciplinary boundaries.

The greatest debt of all is to my wife, Dusia. Words are wholly inadequate to express the support and inspiration she has given me. I dedicate this book to her.

Further reading

My podcast *Countercurrent* features extended conversations with many of the experts in this book.
See http://apple.co/2n5ROy1

Bereiter, Carl, and Marlene Scardamalia, *Surpassing Ourselves: An Inquiry into the Nature and Implications of Expertise* (Open Court, 1993). This book explores the ideas of routine and adaptive expertise which I outline in Chapter 3.

Collins, Harry, and Robert Evans, *Rethinking Expertise* (University of Chicago Press, 2007). The authors develop ideas around contributory and interactional expertise, which I refer to in this book.

Ericsson, K. A., and N. Charness, 'Expert Performance: Its structure and acquisition', *American Psychologist*, 49:8 (1994), 725–47. K. Anders Ericsson's work has been highly influential. This paper gives a flavour of the principles he has distilled from a lifetime's research.

Graziano, Michael, *The Spaces Between Us: A Story of Neuroscience, Evolution, and Human Nature* (Oxford University Press, 2018). This accessible book summarizes Graziano's decades-long research into the neuroscientific basis of personal space.

Johnstone, Keith, *Impro: Improvisation and the Theatre* (Methuen Drama, 1981). A classic work on improvisation – witty, perceptive and easy to read. In it, Johnstone explains the crucial difference between 'Yes, *and* . . .' and 'Yes, *but* . . .' in improvisation.

Lave, Jean, and Etienne Wenger, *Situated Learning: Legitimate Peripheral Participation* (Cambridge University Press, 1991). This influential and accessible book develops the proposition that learning takes place in the context in which it is applied.

McGilchrist, Iain, *The Master and His Emissary: The Divided Brain and the Making of the Western World* (Yale University Press, 2009). This riveting and persuasive book explores the relationship between the differing world views of the right and left sides of the brain.

Meyer, Jan, and Ray Land, *Threshold Concepts and Troublesome Knowledge: Linkages to Ways of Thinking and Practising within the Disciplines* (Enhancing Teaching-Learning Environments in Undergraduate Courses Project, Universities of Edinburgh, Coventry and Durham, 2003). Threshold concepts are a useful way of thinking about learning, and this report sets out the fundamental principles.

Neighbour, Roger, *The Inner Consultation* (Kluwer Academic Publishers, 1987). This book had a pivotal effect on me when I became a general practitioner. Wise, eclectic and unorthodox, it made me realize the central role of the consultation in medicine.

Pallasmaa, Juhani, *The Thinking Hand: Existential and Embodied Wisdom in Architecture* (John Wiley & Sons, 2009). This short book puts forward challenging and illuminating ideas. In it, the author writes: 'There are still countless skills and an immense stock of unverbalised knowledge around the world, embedded in ageless modes of life and livelihoods, that need to be maintained and restored.'

Pirsig, Robert M., *Zen and the Art of Motorcycle Maintenance* (William Morrow and Company, 1974). This fictionalized autobiography explores the nature of 'Quality' through a motorcycle journey from Minnesota to California. Enormously influential and highly idiosyncratic, it remains both thought-provoking and challenging.

Pye, David, *The Nature and Art of Workmanship* (Cambridge University Press, 1968). This short book sets out Pye's influential ideas, as relevant now as when the book was first published.

Sennett, Richard, *The Craftsman* (Yale University Press, 2008). Sennett, a sociologist and musician, explores the many dimensions of skill through a broad historical sweep and asks what is meant by good work.

Tamariz, Juan, *The Five Points in Magic* (Hermetic Press, 2007). A short book by a leading magician, outlining key principles for capturing and shaping an audience's attention.

Wertsch, James, *Vygotsky and the Social Formation of Mind* (Harvard University Press, 1985). This sets out Vygotsky's thinking and provides an excellent introduction to his influential work.

Wickham, John, *An Open and Shut Case: The Story of Keyhole or Minimally Invasive Surgery* (World Scientific Publishing Company, 2017). This fascinating memoir by a pioneer of keyhole surgery captures his innovative spirit, his gentle wit and his humanity.

Index

Page references in *italics* indicate images.
RK indicates Roger Kneebone.